THE PACIFIC WAR ATLAS
1941 – 1945

first edition
David Smurthwaite

Facts On File®

AN INFOBASE HOLDINGS COMPANY

THE PACIFIC WAR ATLAS 1941–1945

Facts On File, Inc.
460 Park Avenue South
New York NY 10016

Library of Congress Cataloging–in–Publication Data
Smurthwaite, David.
    The Pacific war atlas / David Smurthwaite.
        p.   cm.
    Includes bibliographical references and index.
    ISBN 0–8160–3285–8   — ISBN 0–8180–3286–6 (pbk.)
    1. World War, 1939–1945—Campaigns—Pacific Area. I. Title.
D787.S63   1995   95–12018
940.54'26—dc20

Map, text and jacket design by Arcadia Consultants
Maps and design by Arcadia Consultants

Printed and bound in Italy by Sfera Srl

This is a Cynthia Parzych Publishing book produced by:
Mirabel Books Ltd.
P.O. Box 1214
London SW6 7ES

Photo credits
Courtesy of the Trustees of the Imperial War Museum, London 9 bottom, 13, 22–23, 32 top and bottom, 45, 49 top, 51, 52
bottom, 63, 79, 80, 81, 95, 99, 100, 113, 125, 131 top, 133, 137, 141 top
Courtesy of the Museum of the Staffordshire Regiment 118 top
National Archive/USS Intrepid Museum 17, 22 top, 27, 28, 64, 98, 103, 105, 111, 141 centre
Courtesy of the Director, the National Army Museum, London 9 top, 49 bottom, 52 top, 116, 117, 118 bottom, 119 top, 120
top and bottom, 138, 139
Novosti 14, 141 bottom, 143
US Army Official Photograph 124
US Navy Official Photograph 16
US Naval Institute 7 top and bottom, 21, 38, 60, 61, 70, 72, 74 top and bottom, 83, 88, 91, 110, 112 top and bottom, 119
bottom, 121, 127, 131 bottom, 132

10 9 8 7 6 5 4 3 2 1

Contents

Introduction

World War II remains the greatest conflict in the history of mankind. By its close in 1945 the atomic age had been born and a new climate of fear was to become enshrined as the Cold War. The population losses suffered during the war were quickly made good by a bouyant birthrate, but the political map of the world was changed forever. Western imperial rule in the Far East was thrown into reverse by the turmoil produced by Japan's conquest and occupation of British, Dutch, French, and American (Philippines) colonial possessions. From this turmoil emerged new, if not always free, nations which often found themselves enmeshed in a new form of imperialism through alignment with either the expanding communist world or that of the western democracies. With the exception of Africa, the areas of greatest instability occurred in the Far East and particularly in southeast Asia. The legacy of the war in the Pacific endures.

The dominant theatres of operations during World War II were the Far East and Pacific, and Europe and north Africa. Great Britain, Russia and the United States fought against fascism in the European and African theatres, while Great Britain and the United States, with a last minute entry by the Russians, also fought against Japan in the Far East and Pacific. While these theatres generated their own objectives and momentum, they were not entirely independent. The Allies were forced to perform a balancing act with scarce military resources, attempting to meet the priorities of each theatre as the situation demanded. The war in the Pacific was a war of two broad phases. During the first phase the Japanese were everywhere victorious and the Allies suffered a succession of military defeats involving the loss of much of the territory they had held before December 1941. In the second phase the Allies first checked the Japanese, and then began a sustained offensive which by the end of hostilities had reached the threshold of the Japanese home islands.

The problems of conducting operations in the Far East were magnified by the initial scarcity of resources and by the sheer size of the arena in which the battle was fought. That arena was dominated by the Pacific Ocean. Extending over nearly 69 million square miles, the Pacific covers more than a third of the surface of the globe. It is simply the largest and deepest body of water in the world. As a result, the distances across which operations were conducted were staggering. The United States had developed its main Pacific fleet base at Hawaii but the navy still had to attempt to defend the Philippines 5,000 miles further to the west. San Francisco is 7,000 miles from Australia, while Malaya and Panama, respectively at the western and eastern limits of the arena, are 12,500 miles apart.

Air power rode triumphant from the first moments of the conflict when the Japanese sank the battleships of the Pacific Fleet in Pearl Harbor, to the final moments of the war when a B-29 named *Enola Gay* ushered in the nuclear era with a single atomic bomb released over Hiroshima. Yet for all the sophisticated technology deployed in the war in the Pacific, much of the fighting on land revolved around an almost stone age form of combat, prosecuted at close quarters and with the utmost ferocity. At sea the Pacific witnessed the most intensive period of naval warfare in the twentieth century.

The historiography of the Pacific War has been largely undisturbed by serious controversy, except in relation to two events: the attack on Pearl Harbor and the use of the atomic bomb against Japan. The larger-than-life personalities of the Pacific War, men such as Generals MacArthur and Stilwell or Admirals King and Yamamoto, have also aroused debate concerning their influence on national strategy. Yet above all the war in the Pacific is about the ordinary men and women who came from many nations and many walks of life to fight and die for their country or their beliefs.

David Smurthwaite
London, 1995

Key to Maps

National colours

■	United States
■	Great Britain / Australia / New Zealand and other Commonwealth
■	Japanese
■	Dutch
■	French
■	Chinese
■	Soviet

Military units/types

⊠	Infantry
▭	Armoured
⊖	Airborne/parachute
XXXX / 人 / 20	Airforce command
⚓	Naval base/Naval units
TF 38	Task force
YAMAMOTO	Name of commander
⇥	Artillery

Size of military units

XXXXX ▭	Army group
XXXX ▭	Army
XXX ▭	Corps
XX ▭	Division
X ▭	Brigade
III ▭	Regiment
II ▭	Battalion

General military symbols

▲	Minefield
⬳	Air strip
⊘	Airfield
×	Battlefield
∿∿	Fortifications
✸✿	Explosions/bombing

Symbols (continued)

⊿	Signal tower
✦	Fighter
✦	Bomber
↘	Ship sunk
▬	Submarine
▬	Aircraft carrier
▭ 8	Fleet carrier/alternative
▭ 4	Light carrier
⬱	Battleship
⬱	Crusier
⬱	Destroyer
⬱	Other warship
⬬	Transport
→	Movement
⇢	Retreat
▬	Front line
✕	Fighter flight path
✕	Bomber flight path

Other symbols used on maps

▪	Fort
●	Town
○	Capital city
▲	Oilfield
═	Bridge
▲	Mountain
⌒	Rivers
▬	Seas and lakes
⌒	Roads
┄	Rail
—	Borders

1 The Road to War 1918–1941

The United States was a comparative latecomer to the process of establishing influence and gaining territory in the Pacific. Great Britain, France and Holland had already acquired a number of new colonies when the United States finally began to pursue its own interests in the region seriously. In 1867, with the purchase from Russia of Alaska and the Aleutians, the US Pacific coastline was extended by thousands of miles, and the acquisition of the islands of Midway and Samoa pushed American influence out to the west and south. Even so, the territorial gains made by the United States did not reach their peak until the end of the nineteenth century with the annexation of Hawaii, the Philippines and Guam in 1898. The completion of the Panama Canal by American engineers in 1914, and with it control of the shortest shipping route from the Atlantic to the Pacific, finally signalled the emergence of the United States as a two ocean power.

Japan increasingly viewed foreign intrusion into the Pacific with hostility, and during the years 1875-1880 she responded by occupying the Ryukyu, Bonin and Kurile Islands. Using her growing naval and military strength Japan also began to seek further territory at the expense of her neighbours, and especially China. Following war with China in 1894–1895, the Japanese acquired Formosa and the Pescadores Islands and in the glow of Japan's victory over Russia in 1904 they extended their influence in Korea, annexing the country five years later. As Japan worked to consolidate her position in southern Manchuria, the world was forced to acknowledge a new and significant power in the Far East.

The first aircraft carrier to enter the United States Navy was the USS *Langley* (CV 1). Converted from the fleet collier Jupiter between 1920 and 1922, the *Langley* was sunk while ferrying aircraft to Java early in 1942.

On 6 April 1917, the US declared war on Germany and entered World War I as an associate of Great Britain, France, Italy and Russia. The United States also shared common cause with Japan who had joined the struggle against Germany in 1914. While the US sought the defeat of Germany, and was instrumental in the Allied victory, it had no territorial ambitions. Japan, in contrast, had taken the opportunity of the conflict in Europe to coerce China into granting extensive commercial privileges and had occupied Germany's possessions in the Pacific, north of the Equator, when war broke out. By the Treaty of Versailles signed in June 1919, and despite strong American opposition, Japan retained control of Germany's former possessions in the Mariana, Caroline, and Marshall Islands under a League of Nations mandate. These territorial gains propelled Japanese influence some 3,000 miles across the central Pacific and jeopardised the ability of the US to defend the Philippines in any future conflict with Japan. At the same time the British Commonwealth secured similar mandates over former German colonies. Thus Australia was responsible for northeast New Guinea and the Bismarck Archipelago, while New Zealand controlled the German Samoan Islands. A mandate for Nauru was to be administered jointly by Australia, New Zealand, and Great Britain. There were now three principal powers in the Pacific: Great Britain, Japan and the United States.

In the aftermath of World War I the United States faced new and compelling defence problems in the Pacific, but at first she was uncertain as to whether Great Britain or Japan posed the greatest threat to her interests and security. Many American naval officers believed that Great Britain's historic dominance of the oceans should be challenged as a matter of course,

With the six partially constructed battle cruisers of the *Lexington* Class threatened with destruction at the Washington Naval Conference, the United States decided to convert two of these ships into aircraft carriers. One of the vessels chosen was the *Saratoga*, then being built at Camden, New Jersey.

but others saw Japan as the more likely enemy. The reorganisation of the US Navy into three separate fleets in July 1920, deployed respectively in the Atlantic, the Pacific, and in Asia, underlined the fear that the west coast of the United States might require protection from the hostile intentions of Japan. This belief was further demonstrated by the allocation of the latest and most powerful US battleships to the Pacific at the end of 1922. The battlefleet, however, needed shore bases to sustain it and throughout the 1920s the navy pressed for the construction of suitable port and logistics facilities in San Francisco, Puget Sound, and Hawaii. In an effort to persuade Congress to vote the necessary funds, supporters of

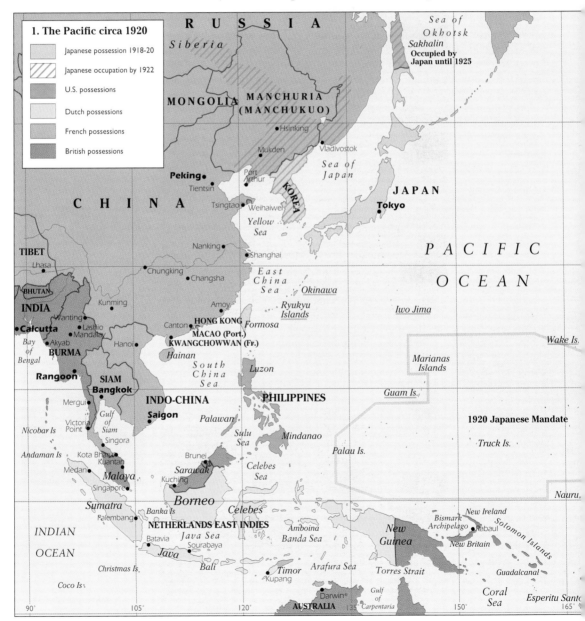

1. The Pacific circa 1920

	Japanese possession 1918–20
	Japanese occupation by 1922
	U.S. possessions
	Dutch possessions
	French possessions
	British possessions

the navy drew a picture of Japan as the menace which the United States, sooner or later, would have to face.

Fearful of an expansionist Japan and at the same time anxious at the cost of a naval building programme, the United States sponsored an international conference in Washington, starting in November 1921, in the hope that the Great Powers might move towards general disarmament, or that treaty limitations could be imposed which would curb a naval arms race. With the elimination of the German Fleet the British Commonwealth remained the strongest naval power, followed by the United States and Japan respectively. For Great Britain, however, weakened militarily and

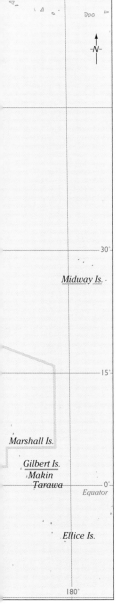

Men of the Scottish Company of the Shanghai Volunteer Corps on active duty in 1927. Troops raised from the local expatriot communities were used to guard western enclaves against the warring factions in China.

Japanese infantry advancing on Chinese forces in Manchuria in 1931 supported by a light tank.

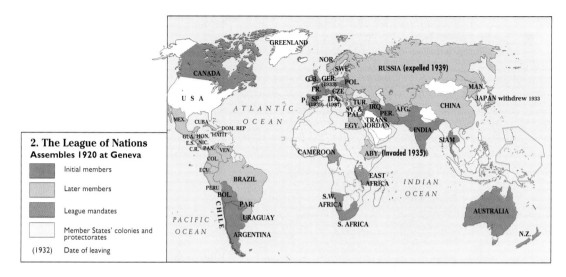

2. The League of Nations
Assembles 1920 at Geneva

- Initial members
- Later members
- League mandates
- Member States' colonies and protectorates
- (1932)   Date of leaving

financially by four years of war, the possibility of maintaining supremacy over a growing United States Navy was no longer a realistic option. At best, Great Britain might achieve, through negotiation, naval equality with the United States and limited superiority over Japan.

For disarmament to work the Washington Conference of 1921–1922 had to find solutions to two outstanding political problems: the Anglo-Japanese Alliance and the future of China. The original defence treaty between Japan and Great Britain, signed in 1902, had been renewed for ten years in 1911 and was thus due to expire. A further renewal of the Alliance could only be interpreted as an act directed against the United States. Great Britain had no desire to be drawn into any future hostilities between Japan and The United States on the Japanese side, but nor did she wish a unilateral abrogation of the Alliance to lead to Japan's seizure of British interests in the Far East. An expedient which rendered the Anglo-Japanese Alliance obsolete had to be found. The answer came in the form of a proposal that the Alliance should be replaced by a treaty between Japan, France, Great Britain and the United States. The Four-Power Treaty signed in December 1921 was a confirmation of the territorial *status quo* in the Pacific, with provision also for the joint settlement of disputes and for joint action against outside aggression. The problem of China took longer to resolve and a generally acceptable solution was not reached until February 1922 with the signing of the Nine Power Treaty. This required those countries, including Japan, with an interest in China to respect that nation's sovereignty and territorial integrity. With agreement in the political sphere progress could be made on the narrower question of limiting naval armaments.

In assessing the relative strength of the maritime powers the standard adopted was predominantly the number and armament of the opposing capital ships (battleships and battlecruisers). This principle was pursued tenaciously by the US Navy despite the fact that not a single shot had been fired in anger by an American battleship during World War I. Passing over the inconclusive result of the Battle of Jutland in 1916, when the British and German battlefleets had failed to decide the course of World War I in an afternoon, naval planners still regarded a big gun fleet action as the decisive phase of any future war at sea. Accordingly, the Washington Five Power Treaty signed in February 1922 between the United States, Great Britain, France, Italy and Japan sought to avoid a naval armaments race by imposing limits, principally, on capital ships.

The signatories to the Washington Treaty agreed that, with the exception of specified replacement tonnage, they would not build any new capital ship for a period of ten years from November 1921. Moreover, Great Britain and the United States were allowed to retain only 20 and 18 capital ships, respectively, from their existing fleets while Japan kept 10. This was a tonnage ratio for battleships and battlecruisers of 525,000 tons for Great Britain and the United States and 315,000 tons for Japan: the famous 5:5:3 formula. France and Italy were limited to battlefleets of 175,000 tons each. The ratios meant that the three larger powers would have to scrap nearly two million tons of battleships or some sixty-six vessels. The Treaty also specified that any new battleship would be limited to a maximum displacement of 35,000 tons (27,000 for battlecruisers) and to a main armament no larger in calibre than 16-inch. Cruisers were limited to 10,000 tons and guns of 8-inch calibre, while aircraft carriers, still regarded as experimental by the Washington Conference, would normally have a maximum displacement of 27,000 tons each. Restrictions of 135,000 tons for the United States and Great Britain, 81,000 for Japan and 60,000 each for France and Italy were placed on carrier tonnage per nation.

Although the Washington Conference failed to make any progress on questions of land and air disarmament its naval agreements, reasserted and extended by the London Naval Treaty of April 1930, remained binding until 31 December 1936. By emphasising the dominance of the battleship, and relegating aircraft and submarines to secondary roles, the treaty exercised a signal influence on the world's most powerful navies until the eve of World War II. At Washington Great Britain had effectively surrendered her traditional supremacy on the high seas and by so doing had all but removed the possibility of future war with the United States. The tonnage ratios embodied in the treaty also meant that the Royal Navy would find it almost impossible to fight a simultaneous war in European and Far Eastern waters without a powerful ally. The United States appeared to have come well out of the Conference for although it had only eighteen capital ships to Great Britain's twenty, her battleships were in general faster and more modern than those of the Royal Navy. Also the United States was allowed by the treaty, as was Japan, to convert two battlecruiser hulls into 33,000 ton aircraft carriers. This resulted in the *Saratoga* and the *Lexington*; the finest carriers of their type in the world when commissioned in 1927.

There was a sting in the tail of the Washington Conference. The Japanese, in return for agreeing to an unfavourable tonnage ratio of capital ships, had secured a clause in the Five Power Treaty which banned the enhancement or construction of fortifications and naval bases in the western Pacific. In Great Britain's case this ban affected Hong Kong but not Singapore, and for the United States all possessions west of Hawaii and the Aleutians. For Japan it meant the non-fortification of the Bonin, Kurile, and Ryukyu Islands, Formosa and the Pescadores.

Although limiting the naval strength of the Great Powers was an important step towards curbing armaments, it was not the only initiative taken to promote lasting peace. President Wilson's main ambition at the Versailles peace talks had been to promote a League of Nations to safeguard the

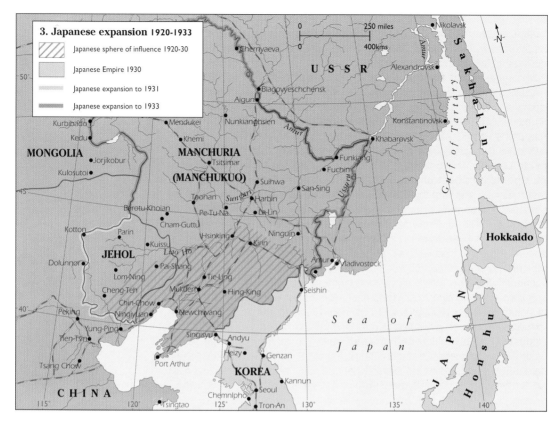

3. Japanese expansion 1920-1933

- Japanese sphere of influence 1920-30
- Japanese Empire 1930
- Japanese expansion to 1931
- Japanese expansion to 1933

world against aggression. Once the Covenant of the League was established, however, the United States Senate refused to ratify the Treaty of Versailles and the United States returned to a policy of isolation. The League of Nations, as a result, had to strive to meet the problems of the post-war era without the assistance of one of the most powerful nations on earth. The first far-reaching challenge to the League and its objectives came in the Far East and from one of the signatories to the Covenant – Japan.

By 1931 Japan was in the grip of a financial and social crisis. Supported by a post-war economic boom the Japanese population had been growing at a rate close to one million a year and it had now far outstripped the capacity of the nation's own resources. If Japan was to continue to prosper foreign markets were essential, but the Depression in the United States severely affected Japan's silk trade and resurgent nationalism in China struck at the flow of vital imports and exports. As hardship spread amongst the agricultural landowners and workers of Japan the army gained increasing support for its own forthright solutions. Manchuria was part of China, but Japan had invested heavily in its economy and the Japanese military were not prepared to stand idly by while this investment was in jeopardy. Since troops were already stationed in China to protect Japanese installations, the army also had the means with which to act.

On 18 September 1931 the Japanese Kwantung Army, citing as its justification a Chinese attack on the South Manchurian Railway near Mukden, ignored the wishes of the Japanese government and set in motion plans for the occupation of the whole of Manchuria. Protests by the League of Nations and the United States at the subsequent creation of the Japanese puppet state of Manchukuo merely led to Japan's eventual withdrawal from the League in 1933. Internationally isolated, Japan grew increasingly xenophobic. The end of the Gold Standard in December 1931, however, had resulted in a massive devaluation of the yen and a consequent boom in the Japanese economy. Fuelled by increased government spending, growth continued at an impressive rate and expenditure on Japan's armed services rose proportionately, reinforcing the military's hold on national policy.

By 1936 that policy had crystallised into three main requirements: Japan had to be prepared to counter Russian pressure from the north; she must attempt the conquest of China; and she had to expand to the south and east to secure the wealth and raw materials needed to support her military effort. Great Britain, China, France, Holland, Russia and the United States could be expected to oppose this policy. Japan therefore needed to strengthen her military and economic position and secure whatever assistance she could. In November 1936 a Japanese-German agreement, principally directed against Russia and known as the Anti-Comintern Pact, was signed. A year later Italy too joined the Pact.

While tension between Japan and China remained high, actual fighting, such as that which had broken out at Shanghai early in 1932 and in the Chinese province of Jehol in 1933, had arisen from isolated and separate incidents. In July 1937, however, Japan launched an all-out, though undeclared, war on China and began the conquest of the central and northern regions of the country in earnest. In the north Japanese progress was swift but further south bitter Chinese resistance, particularly around Shanghai,

Japanese troops marching through the Gate of Peiping in September 1937.

meant that the twin Japanese thrusts did not link up until the capture of Tungshan in May 1938. Despite these gains the Japanese still did not have a secure hold on the country, and the Chinese Nationalist leader Chiang Kai-shek continued the government of unoccupied China from Chungking in Szechwan. In an effort to isolate Chunking from overseas aid the Japanese mounted amphibious landings between February and April 1941 to occupy the southern ports of China.

Japan's attempts to gain territory at the expense of Russia had led to convincing victories for the Red Army in clashes on the Manchurian and Korean borders but, with Great Britain and France at war with Germany, Japan felt confident in her ability to secure concessions in Indo-China. After the defeat of Holland and France in the summer of 1940 Japan attempted to exert pressure on the Dutch to maintain supplies of raw materials from the East Indies, and sent troops to occupy the north of French Indo-China. In September 1940, in what was a clear warning to the United States to remain neutral, Japan entered into a defensive alliance with Germany and Italy through the Tripartite Pact. The Soviet–Japanese non-aggression pact of April 1941, together with the German attack on the Soviet Union in June, eased Japan's fears of an attack from the north and gave her the strategic freedom to exploit developments in the south. The key problem for the Japanese was how to achieve the southern advance without provoking the United States into declaring war.

Since June 1938 the United States had attempted to deter Japan's aggression through measures which would curb her economic and military power. These included restrictions on the export to Japan of commodities and equipment that were potentially useful in war, the freezing of Japanese assets in the United States, and increased aid to Chiang Kai-shek and the Chinese nationalists. Later the British and Dutch followed the lead of the United States and by the summer of 1941 Japan faced an almost total embargo on strategic imports including oil. The Japanese regarded this policy as an unfriendly act and responded by declaring their intention to found a new order in Asia, the Greater East Asian Co-Prosperity Sphere. This would be a Japanese controlled political and economic grouping which would be organised to supply the raw materials that Japan needed and to take exports in return. Amongst the countries Japan proposed to include in this new order were Australia, India, Burma, Malaya, the Philippines, New Guinea, New Zealand and Thailand. Any nation objecting to its inclusion in the Sphere would be dealt with as an enemy.

The American embargoes meant that effectively the Japanese were

Three of the Russian commanders who were responsible for the success of Red Army operations against the Japanese on the Manchurian Border in 1939. On the left is Corps Commander Georgi Zhukov who in 1941 became Chief of the General Staff and later rose to the rank of Marshal of the Soviet Union.

trapped. If they could not find new supplies their strategic reserves of oil would last for little more than two years at current consumption. Thus the choice appeared to be either submission to American demands that China and the Greater East Asian Co-Prosperity Sphere be relinquished, or the use of military force to secure new sources of oil and raw materials. Neither the American people nor their president wanted war with Japan and the majority of Japanese wished, if possible, to avoid outright conflict with the United States. Unfortunately, the conditions required by the two nations to reach a workable solution to their difficulties were diametrically opposed. Japan would not leave China; the United States said that she must. To many Japanese it now seemed that the only alternative to expansion was decline.

Japan was propelled into war in part, at least, by the reluctance of the Powers to acknowledge the problems of individual countries and by their failure to work together to find solutions. Mutual suspicion, economic rivalry, and the desire for territorial expansion created a climate in the 1930s which allowed national problems to become international flash-points. As peaceful initiatives failed the influence of the armed forces, and particularly the dominance of the army, spread through Japanese society and politics. This influence first brought war with China in 1937 and then war with the western democracies in 1941.

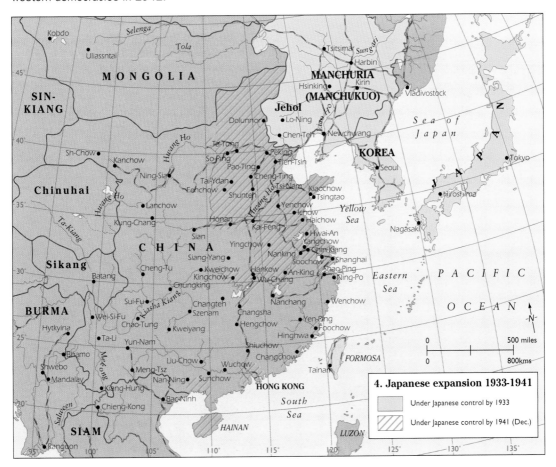

4. Japanese expansion 1933-1941

Under Japanese control by 1933

Under Japanese control by 1941 (Dec.)

2 Pearl Harbor to Hong Kong

The final decision to go to war with the United States, Great Britain and Holland was taken in Tokyo on 1 December 1941. Six days later at 7.49 am on Sunday 7 December (Hawaiian time) the first wave of an aerial armada of Japanese fighters, bombers and torpedo planes swooped down upon the ships of the US Pacific Fleet at anchor in Pearl Harbor. Within minutes many of the US Navy's most powerful battleships were engulfed in flames, their hulls ripped open by torpedos and their superstructures shattered by armour-piercing bombs. As the aircraft carriers which had launched the Japanese strike planes began their withdrawal to home waters, much of the Pacific Fleet lay in apparent ruin at the bottom of Pearl Harbor.

A daring Japanese strategy, carried out with courage and supreme professionalism, had at a stroke seized the initiative in the Pacific. Yet that strategy had been fraught with risk and it had been imposed upon a sceptical and unwilling navy by the strength and dedication of a single officer, Fleet Admiral Isoroku Yamamoto. It came almost as a last minute expedient and it overturned the Japanese Navy's traditional view of how a war at sea against the United States should be fought.

Since the early twentieth century the Japanese Navy had planned for a conflict against the United States. Naval strategists, assuming that Japan would be engaged in a war with this single enemy, proposed that the battlefleet should fight an essentially defensive campaign in waters close to the home islands. Japanese warship designers had produced fast and powerfully armed vessels that sacrificed standards of crew accommodation, defensive armour, and range. A single extra torpedo tube, gun, or knot of speed would, it was thought, make individual ships superior to their

Fleet Admiral Isoroku Yamamoto, Commander-in-Chief of the Combined Fleet from 1939 to 1943 was a central figure in the Japanese Navy's operations in the Pacific.

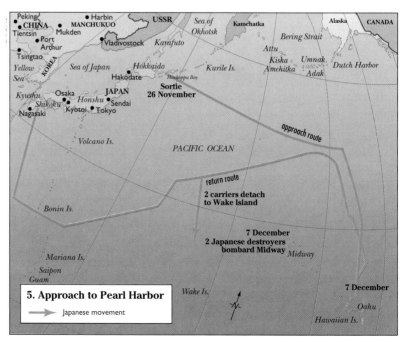

5. Approach to Pearl Harbor

American equivalents in the fleet battle that would secure victory.

While the navy held to this course, Japanese strategic planning as a whole was complicated during the interwar years by uncertainty as to whether Russia or the United States would be the eventual enemy. If Japan expanded to the north then she could expect to clash with Russia; if she expanded to the south her principal opponents would be the United States and Great Britain. As a result while the navy prepared for war in the Pacific, the army prepared for war in Asia. In August 1936 Japan took the fatal step of adopting these competing strategies as national policy, so provoking not

Below: The magazine of the destroyer USS *Shaw* explodes after the ship was hit by bombs from Japanese aircraft at Pearl Harbor in 1941.

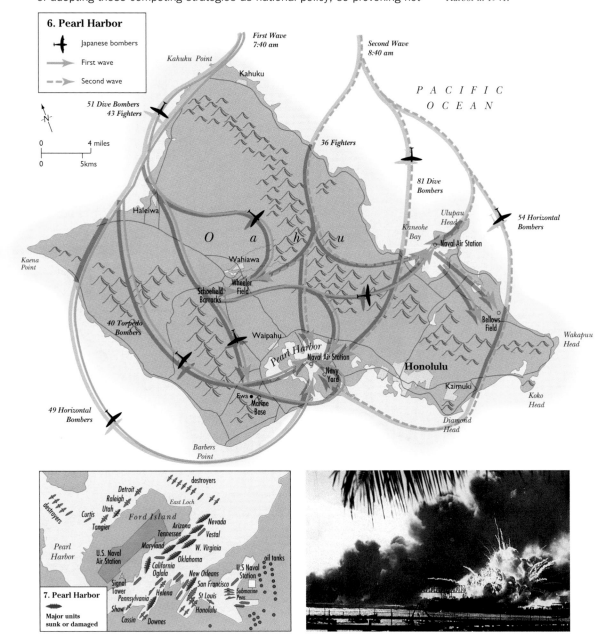

6. Pearl Harbor

Japanese bombers

First wave

Second wave

51 Dive Bombers
43 Fighters

0   4 miles
0   5kms

First Wave
7:40 am

Second Wave
8:40 am

Kahuku Point

Kahuku

*P A C I F I C
O C E A N*

36 Fighters

81 Dive
Bombers

Ulupau
Head

54 Horizontal
Bombers

Kaneohe
Bay

Naval Air Station

Haleiwa

O   a   h   u

Kaena
Point

Wahiawa

Wheeler
Field

Schofield
Barracks

40 Torpedo
Bombers

Waipahu

Pearl Harbor
Naval Air Station

Navy
Yard

Honolulu

Bellows
Field

Wakapuu
Head

Kaimuki

Koko
Head

Ewa •
Marine
Base

49 Horizontal
Bombers

Diamond
Head

Barbers
Point

7. Pearl Harbor

Major units
sunk or damaged

destroyers

Detroit
Raleigh
Utah

East Loch

destroyers

Curtis
Tangier

Ford Island

Nevada

Pearl
Harbor

U.S. Naval
Air Station

Arizona
Tennessee

Vestal

Maryland

W. Virginia

California
Oglala

Oklahoma

New Orleans

U.S Naval
Station

oil tanks

Signal
Tower
Pennsylvania

Helena

San Francisco

St Louis

Submarine
Pens

Shaw

Honolulu

Cassin   Downes

only an arms race but also the continuing hostility of both the United States and the Soviet Union.

The navy's final break with a short range strategy designed purely to respond to an attack by an aggressor, was due to the increasing probability that Japan would become engaged in a world war. The military alliance with the Axis pitted Japan in the Far East against the United States, Great

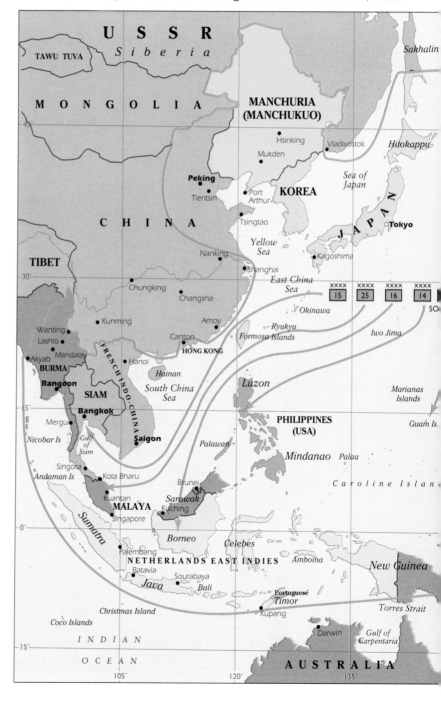

Britain and Holland in addition to China. This meant fighting a large-scale, long-drawn out conflict in which the possession of ample raw materials would be vital. To have a chance of victory Japan had to be certain of adequate oil supplies and these were to be found in southeast Asia. Yet the US Pacific Fleet based at Hawaii represented a grave and present threat to any campaign of conquest in the southern area.

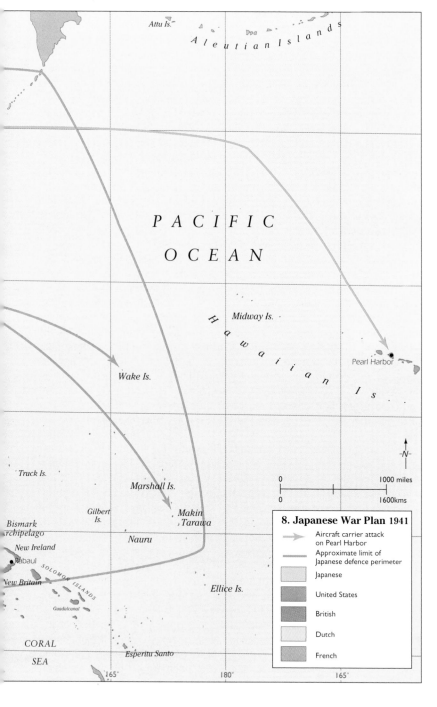

8. Japanese War Plan 1941

- Aircraft carrier attack on Pearl Harbor
- Approximate limit of Japanese defence perimeter
- Japanese
- United States
- British
- Dutch
- French

That the United States Navy had retained the potential to defeat Japan at sea while also fighting in European waters was due in large measure to two men; Congressman Carl Vinson who became Chairman of the House Naval Affairs Committee in 1930, and Franklin Delano Roosevelt who was elected President in March 1933. Roosevelt understood the navy as well as, or better, than any previous President and he was a firm supporter of its long-term reconstruction. Vinson was a dedicated advocate of a balanced navy comprising battleships, carriers, and submarines, and he worked closely with Secretary of the Navy Claude A Swanson to build a fleet that could meet the commitments of the United States across two oceans.

The navy had been restricted in size and type of ship by the Washington and London Treaties of 1922 and 1930, but successive administrations had failed to ensure that construction was maintained even within these limits. Vinson, together with Senator Alexander Trammel, reversed this policy in March 1934 when the President signed what became known as the Vinson-Trammel Act. This authorised a construction programme of some 730 naval aircraft and 70 new warships in the years 1935–1939, subject to congressional funding. In May 1938 the 'Second Vinson Act' made provision for an increase in authorised naval tonnage of 23 per cent and the completion of an additional 950 naval aircraft. In July 1940 the US Navy's strength of 2,000 ships and 1,750 aircraft was enhanced by the Vinson-Walsh Two Ocean Navy Act which authorised a further 20 per cent increase in ships and a total naval air fleet of 15,000 aircraft.

Vinson's measures thoroughly alarmed the Japanese who believed that the delicate balance of the 7:7:5 ratio of capital ship tonnage which, with the United States' reluctance to build, had largely worked in their favour would now swing strongly against them. When the treaty limitations expired in December 1936, Japan began another period of naval expansion under the Marusan Programme. This programme emphasised a need for a fleet of superior quality and armament to that of the United States to compensate for Japan's numerical inferiority in ships. As a result the 'super-battleships' *Musashi* and *Yamato*, the largest and most heavily armed capital ships in the world, were laid down under this programme. By 1941 Japan's combat fleet had more than doubled since 1922 to reach a total of 1,059,000 tons, compared to a tonnage for the US Navy of 1,550,000, afloat or building.

By the beginning of 1941 Admiral Yamamoto, then Commander-in-Chief of the Combined Fleet, was convinced, despite the rearmament programme, that the Japanese Navy could not successfully wage an all-out war against the United States for more than a year. Nor did he accept that the American Fleet would wait for Japan to carry through its conquests in the south before launching its own attack. The cautious strategy followed by the Japanese Navy General Staff, which committed the navy solely to the southern advance, would, he believed, lead only to disaster. Yamamoto was certain that Japan must attempt to cripple the naval strength of the United States at the same moment as she launched her thrust to the south. He therefore proposed the bold concept of attacking the Pacific Fleet in its base at Pearl Harbor at the very start of hostilities.

Yamamoto instructed Rear Admiral Takijiro Onishi, Chief of Staff of the 11th Air Fleet, to assess the feasibility of an attack on Pearl Harbor. Onishi was a career aviator who saw at once that for an attack to succeed it would have to be based on a strike by the aircraft carriers of the 1st Air Fleet.

Japan's land-based air power could take off no nearer to Hawaii than the Marshal Islands, which lay some 2,000 miles from Pearl Harbor, – an impossible distance for a bombing raid. Accordingly, Onishi enlisted the aid of Commander Minoru Genda, an outstanding staff officer and tactician who was serving with the 1st Air Fleet.

Genda's detailed study of the operation showed that a successful attack could be made on Pearl Harbor, but only if certain essential conditions were met. Genda stipulated that complete secrecy must be maintained to ensure surprise; that only well-qualified pilots and the most able commanders should be selected for the operation; and that all six of the navy's large carriers must be deployed for the attack. The Navy General Staff were highly critical of the operation, believing that to divert the carriers to strike at Hawaii would leave the southern advance dangerously exposed. They were also doubtful that secrecy could be maintained and surprise achieved since the task force would spend a month at sea before its planes reached their launch point. In the end Yamamoto only overcame their opposition by threatening to resign as the Commander-in-Chief of the Combined Fleet if the Pearl Harbor attack did not go ahead. On 3 November 1941, only thirty-five days before Japanese bombs and torpedos tore into the battleships of the Pacific Fleet, Admiral Nagano, Chief of the Navy General Staff, gave his approval for the operation. Almost at a stroke Japanese naval strategy for a Pacific war had changed from defence into attack.

By the beginning of December 1941 the Japanese Fleet could deploy ten battleships, ten aircraft carriers, eight heavy and eighteen light cruisers, 113 destroyers, and sixty-three submarines. From this powerful force six

Congressman Carl Vinson, Chairman of the House Naval Affairs Committee during much of the 1930's, was an effective advocate of a powerful United States Navy which could meet its commitments in both the Pacific and the Atlantic.

large carriers (Carrier Divisions 1, 2, and 5) plus a screen of two battle-ships (Battleship Division 3), two heavy cruisers (Cruiser Division 8), and one light cruiser and nine destroyers (Destroyer Squadron 1) would be detached for the strike against Pearl Harbor. A refuelling fleet of eight tankers accompanied the task force while three submarines would scout 200 miles ahead. In additon two destroyers (Destroyer Division 7) were tasked to bombard Midway Island, while twenty-six submarines (Submarine Squadrons 1, 2, and 3) would blockade Hawaii. The task force was under the overall command of Vice Admiral Chuichi Nagumo and the air attack force was led by Captain Mitsuo Fuchida.

Of crucial importance to the success of the operation was the route which was to be taken by the task force as it covered more than 3,000 nautical miles on its approach to Pearl Harbor. If the fleet was spotted at sea by a single enemy or neutral ship with a radio on board then in all prob-ability surprise would be lost. To minimise this risk the task force would sail east across the Pacific by a northerly route, thus avoiding commercial sea lanes and the airborne patrols from Wake and Midway, before turning south towards Oahu. Even on this route many problems remained, not least the difficulty of refuelling the destroyers at sea when meteorological records showed that on only seven days during the voyage would conditions be suitable for such operations.

After preparing for sea at Kure Naval Station the ships of the Japanese task force sailed in groups to an appointed rendezvous in Tankan (Hitokappu) Bay on the south coast of Etorofu Island in the Kuriles on 22 November. The fleet was now informed of its mission and at 6.00 am on 26 November the carriers *Akagi*, *Hiryu*, *Kaga*, *Shokaku*, *Soryu*, and *Zuikaku*, together with the battleships *Hiei* and *Kirishima* and their supporting ships, weighed anchor and slipped out into the dark, fog-shrouded waters of the

Far left: An aerial view of Pearl Harbor as seen through the lens of a camera carried by a Japanese aircraft on 7 December 1941. Battleship row is visible in the middle left of the picture.

The Japanese aircraft carrier *Shokaku* was one of the six fleet carriers that launched aircraft against Pearl Harbor. The *Shokaku* was sunk by the US submarine *Cavalla* on 19 June 1944.

north Pacific amidst strict radio silence. Their first objective was a stand-by point more than 1,000 miles to the north of Oahu at latitude 42°N longitude 170°W, where the task force would receive final confirmation to proceed with the attack or an instruction to return home. On 2 December the coded signal 'Climb Mount Niitaka' was received by the task force. Hostilities with the United States would begin on 8 December (Tokyo time) and it was to proceed with the attack on Pearl Harbor.

President Roosevelt and a small circle of officials in his administration were fully aware that Japan was on the brink of war. The Japanese diplomatic code, known as 'Purple', had been broken by the United States in September 1940 and this information, together with radio interception traffic, was designated by the codeword MAGIC. Once American Intelligence could decrypt 'Purple' it was able to read signals between Tokyo and the Japanese Embassies in Berlin and Washington. Roosevelt knew that Tokyo had ordered the Japanese Ambassador, Admiral Kichisaburo Nomura, and Special Envoy Saburo Kurusu, to reach an agreement on Japanese-American differences by 29 November 1941, warning that thereafter 'things are automatically going to happen'. On 30 November a signal from Tokyo to its embassy in Berlin contained an instruction to inform the German High Command that:

'There is extreme danger that war may suddenly break out between the Anglo-Saxon nations and Japan through some clash of arms and add that the time of the breaking out of this war may come quicker than anyone dreams.'

Assessments of Japan's intentions, based on MAGIC, normally concluded that the immediate threat would be to the Philippines and to British and Dutch possessions in southeast Asia, rather than to Pearl Harbor. The US Navy war warning of 27 November 1941, which stressed that an 'aggressive move by Japan is expected within the next few days', alerted commands to the probability of enemy operations against Borneo, the Kra Peninsula, or the Philippines, but did not mention Hawaii.

The Japanese naval code known as 'JN-25' proved to be a more difficult target and while both the Americans in Manila and the British at Singapore were intercepting the code, they were able to decipher less than 10 per cent of this traffic. Even so from the beginning of November American Intelligence began to suspect that the Japanese Navy was involved in something unusual. Japanese submarines were traced moving east, fleet concentrations in the south were located through radio traffic analysis, and the experts in Hawaii lost track of the aircraft carriers completely. What little progress had been made with 'JN-25' came to a complete halt on 1 December 1941 when a new Japanese naval code 'J-25b' was introduced. As Nagumo prepared to launch his planes 300 miles to the north of Oahu on 7 December, the US Navy Department listed the Japanese carriers and their accompanying warships as anchored at the naval stations at Kure and Sasebo on the main islands of Honshu and Kyushu.

Drawing the correct conclusions from top secret intelligence when, for security reasons, individual decrypts cannot be retained or analysed at length by specially trained staff is a task fraught with difficulty. Moreover, the need to preserve the source of the intelligence meant that information was circulated to command posts on a very limited basis. While all the recipients of MAGIC could see that Japan was going to war, no one linked the enemy's naval preparations with an immediate attack on Pearl Harbor. Indeed the threat to the Pacific Fleet, if indeed one existed, was felt to be from submarines or from sabotage to installations on Oahu. Accordingly Lieutenant General Walter C Short, commanding the army units in Hawaii, and Admiral Husband Kimmel, Commander-in-Chief of the US Fleet and Pacific Fleet, took steps to counter these twin dangers.

On 4 December when Nagumo and his ships were some 900 miles north of Midway, they turned southeast and steamed to a point approximately 500 miles north of Oahu. The Japanese task force fuelled at sea on 6 and 7 December (Tokyo time) screened by a low, dense cloud-base. The tankers then departed and the carriers, which were sailing in parallel columns of three, with the battleships and heavy cruisers on the flank, increased speed from fourteen to twenty-four knots and turned south. The light cruiser and the destroyers provided an outer defensive circle as the task force began its final run to the launch point for the carrier planes.

One major imponderable remained; would the Pacific Fleet be in Pearl Harbor or at sea on exercise? Japanese intelligence 'A' information issued at 6.00 pm on 7 December (Tokyo time) stated that nine battleships, seven light cruisers, twenty destroyers, and three seaplane tenders were in harbour. Of the ultimate prize, the American aircraft carriers, there was no trace. Despite this setback the Japanese pilots and crewmen of the task force took comfort in the fact that nine battleships would fall victim to their bombs and torpedos. In the event, the intelligence summary proved incorrect in a number of particulars and there were actually ninety-four American warships and auxiliary vessels in Pearl Harbor. The major combat vessels comprised eight not nine battleships – *Arizona*, *California*, *Maryland*, *Nevada*, *Oklahoma*, *Pennsylvania*, *Tennessee*, and *West Virginia*, two heavy cruisers, six light cruisers, twenty-nine destroyers and five submarines. The Japanese believed that four carriers – *Enterprise*, *Hornet*, *Lexington* and *Yorktown* – were based at Pearl Harbor, although in fact *Hornet* and *Yorktown* were on duty in the Atlantic. The *Saratoga* was to reach Hawaii from San Diego a week after the Japanese attack.

Before dawn on 7 December 1941 (Hawaiian time; 8 December Tokyo time) the Japanese task force reached a position 230 miles due north of Pearl Harbor and prepared to launch its attack force of over 350 planes. At 6.00 am the first wave of 183 torpedo planes, dive bombers, level bombers and fighters took off from the decks of the carriers and headed for the island of Oahu. One hour and forty minutes later Captain Fuchida, having used his radio direction finder to home in on the broadcasts of the Honolulu Radio Station, spotted the island's north shore at Kahuku Point through breaks in the cloud. At 7.49 am Fuchida gave the order to attack and the forty torpedo bombers led by Lieutenant Commander Shigeharu Murata dived towards the battleships anchored to the east of Ford Island. Lieutenant Commander Shigeru Itaya's fighter escort group of forty-three Zeros swept over Oahu in search of enemy planes, while Lieutenant Commander Kakuichi Takahashi's fifty-one Type-99 carrier dive bombers climbed to 12,000 feet. As Fuchida turned his forty-nine Type-97 (Kate) bombers towards Barbers Point there was not a single United States fighter or artillery burst to be seen. Fuchida radioed the signal 'Tora, tora, tora' the code for 'surprise attack successful' to the carrier *Akagi* at 7.53 am.

It was a Sunday morning and the command structure at Pearl Harbor had reacted slowly to indications that all was not well in the vicinity of the Fleet's anchorage. At 3.55 am a sighting of a Japanese midget submarine near to the entrance to the harbour had been passed to Captain William Outerbridge who was commanding the harbour patrol from the destoyer *Ward*. Outerbridge took no action. He did act, however, on a second report three hours later and at 6.45 am the *Ward* sank an enemy submarine that was trying to enter the harbour. Admiral Kimmel was informed of this encounter at 7.10 am but he decided to wait for verification before ordering an alert. At the same time a PBY Catalina flying boat was attacking another midget submarine, but the 14th Naval District Commander Rear Admiral Claude Bloch, to whom the report was made, did not believe it to be urgent. At 7.02 am a mobile army radar set at Opana, near Kahuku Point, reported incoming planes approximately 137 miles to the north of the island. The Army Aircraft Warning Service Information Center on Oahu decided that the radar was tracking a flight of B-17 bombers that was expected from the mainland. The immediate signs of a possible Japanese attack were thus, due to a mixture of complacency and inexperience, treated with a lack of urgency that proved fatal.

Fuchida's first wave bombers and fighters destroyed the majority of the Army Air Corps planes based at Wheeler, Bellows, and Hickham Fields. This was not difficult since as an anti-sabotage measure the aircraft were parked wing-tip to wing-tip and not dispersed around their fields. The Japanese also decimated the naval patrol planes and fighters on Ford Island, the PBY Catalinas at Kaneohe Naval Air Station, and the Marine air wing at Ewa Airfield. The torpedo bombers meanwhile split into two main groups with sixteen planes making for the west side of Pearl Harbor, while a larger group of twenty-four flew to the southeast before turning north over Hickam Field and then northwest to attack Battleship Row. The pilots had orders to drop their new torpedos, especially modified to deal with the shallow waters of Pearl Harbor, only when they were certain of a hit. The battleships moored outboard took the first torpedo strikes. The *West Virginia* and the *Oklahoma* were hit several times, the former, thanks to counter-flooding by an alert crew, settling upright on the shallow bottom, the latter capsizing. The *California* took two torpedo hits and sank to her superstructure, while the *Nevada*, although struck by a torpedo and two bombs, managed to get underway only to run aground later when hit by three more bombs.

The second wave of 171 strike planes which had taken off from the carriers at 7.15 am arrived over Oahu at 8.54 am, and while the fifty-four Type-97 Kate bombers concentrated on the air bases the eighty-one Type-90 dive bombers (Vals), approaching over the east coast mountains, sought out any ships which had escaped the first wave attack. Shore and ship anti-aircraft guns were by now throwing up a formidable barrage but it was not enough to save the in-board battleships. The *Arizona* blew up under a rain of bombs with the loss of over eighty per cent of her crew, and the *Tennessee* and the *Maryland* were badly damaged. The *Pennsylvania*, then in dry dock, was also damaged by a bomb hit.

As the last Japanese planes headed north towards their carriers they left behind a scene of fire and devastation. Eighteen ships of the Pacific Fleet – eight battleships, three light cruisers, three destroyers, and four auxiliary vessels – had been sunk, had capsized, or had been badly damaged. Eighty naval aircraft together with a number of small ships and transports had also been lost. For the Army Air Corps the losses were just as severe with seventy-seven aircraft of all types destroyed and another 128 planes damaged. Including civilians, 2,403 people died in the attack and 1,178 were wounded. The Japanese lost twenty-nine planes to anti-aircraft fire and to the few American fighters that managed to get airborne. At sea one Japanese submarine and five midget submarines were sunk.

Although the officers and men on Oahu were stunned by the devastation around them it could have been far worse. The installations at Hickham, Ford Island, Kaneohe and Wheeler had been badly damaged, but the Pacific Fleet's priceless fuel and ammunition reserves, repairs shops, dry docks, and submarine pens had survived. As the Japanese planes returned to their carriers Admiral Nagumo was urged to order a second attack. The strike power of the Japanese fleet was still intact and Pearl Harbor was now largely undefended. Would there ever be a better opportunity to complete the destruction of Oahu's facilities and stores or to locate and sink the missing American carriers? Nagumo, concerned that his tankers were already withdrawing to the north and that enemy carrier or land-based aircraft might be in the process of mounting a counterattack against his fleet, refused and ordered the task force to set course for home. This failure to exploit the initial success at Pearl Harbor restricted the Japanese Navy's achievement to a tactical victory rather than a longer term strategic gain. The American carriers, heavy cruisers and submarines were still intact and the damage on Oahu was quickly repaired. In failing to destroy these elements of the Pacific Fleet the Japanese had allowed what were to become the most potent weapons of the naval war in the Pacific to escape. In its carriers the United States had a force which, within six months of Pearl Harbor, would throw the Japanese onto the defensive, and in its submarines it had a weapon which would eventually strangle the life blood of Japan's war effort.

Who was to blame for the tragedy at Pearl Harbor? In an attempt to find

The scene at the United States Army aerodrome at Hickham Field after the Japanese bombers had departed. In the foreground is a B-17E Flying Fortress.

a speedy and authoritative answer to this question Roosevelt appointed an investigative commission chaired by Supreme Court Associate Justice Owen J Roberts. Accompanied by two senior officers from both the army and the navy, Roberts began the commission's hearings in Hawaii on 22 December 1941, only two weeks after the attack. On Saturday 24 January 1942 the commission's report was on the president's desk in the White House. The next day, at Roosevelt's express wish, it was published in Sunday newspapers across the United States. The report laid the responsibility for the defeat at Pearl Harbor squarely on the shoulders of Kimmel and Short in terms that were scathing in their clarity: 'The Japanese attack was a complete surprise to the commanders, and they failed to make suitable dispositions to meet such an attack. Each failed properly to evaluate the seriousness of the situation. These errors of judgement were the effective causes for the success of the attack.'

Revisionist historians have since argued that the Robert's Commission was little more than a cover-up designed to protect the guilty in Washington, or to disguise the existence of a conspiracy aimed at taking the United States into the war by provoking a Japanese surprise attack. With these propositions in mind some historians have concluded that Kimmel and Short were in fact innocent of the charges laid against them. While it is possible to agree that the Robert's Commission was too close to the

The pride of the United States Pacific Fleet lies in ruins. The battleships engulfed in flames at Pearl Harbor are from left to right, USS *Maryland*, USS *Tennessee*, USS *Oklahoma*, USS *Arizona*, and USS *West Virginia*.

events it was investigating, and that its judgement that Kimmel and Short were guilty of both 'errors of judgement' and 'dereliction of duty' was too harsh, it is difficult to accept that they can be absolved of responsibility for failing to prepare adequately to meet a Japanese attack. If more fundamental reasons are sought then the true responsibility for this defeat is to be found in the failure of both the army and the navy to absorb and act upon the deadly capabilities of modern air power against ships and their supporting installations.

In political terms Pearl Harbor was a disaster for the Japanese. Although their best intention was to declare war before Fuchida's planes arrived over Hawaii, their diplomats did not do so. Problems at the Japanese Embassy in Washington in decoding the fourteen-part message of 6–7 December 1941 meant that although the final note was eventually delivered to the US State Department, it did not reach the Secretary of State, Cordell Hull, until fifty-five minutes after Japanese planes began hostilities. It is doubtful if the actual timing of the declaration troubled the Japanese Government greatly, but it did characterise Japan in the eyes of much of the world as a sneak aggressor who had indeed committed an act that would 'live in infamy'. Moreover, it united the American people, who until Pearl Harbor were still beset by isolationists and non-interventionists, behind the war effort with an intensity that little else could have achieved. The declaration of war against the United States by Germany and Italy on 11 December 1941 merely fanned the nation's fury.

For Great Britain, the Japanese attack on Pearl Harbor and the United States's entry into the war came as a beacon of hope. When Winston Churchill heard the news of the Japanese attack he was dining at Chequers, his official country residence, with Averell Harriman, President Roosevelt's special envoy. As Churchill recorded later, his sadness at the losses inflicted on the Pacific Fleet was mixed with joy at the certainty of victory now that the United States would be fighting at Great Britain's side.

'So we had won after all! Hitler's fate was sealed. Mussolini's fate was sealed. As for the Japanese, they would be ground to powder. All the rest was merely the proper application of overwhelming force.'

Much remained to be done before victory would be achieved and in the Far East the Japanese were to exact a heavy penalty from an unprepared Great Britain and the United States.

The strike against Pearl Harbor, although considered an essential strategic factor, was only part of Japan's opening campaign. With their navy now in control of the central and western Pacific the Japanese could carry out their plan of conquest without fear of intervention by a superior US Pacific Fleet. On 7 December 1941 (Washington time; 8 December local time), attacks were launched against the Philippines, Hong Kong and Malaya. The American outposts on Guam and Wake were to be occupied along with British Borneo, and once the Philippines and Malaya had fallen the conquest of the Dutch East Indies and Burma would begin. By European standards the resources available to the Japanese for this advance into southeast Asia and the Pacific were comparatively few, especially in the army's case. The majority of the army's fifty-one infantry divisions were required for service in China, Korea and Japan, and to guard against intervention by the Soviet Union. Only some eleven divisions were available for operations elsewhere and they could expect support from barely 2,000 combat aircraft, both army and navy. Yet speed was of the essence for the major campaigns had to be completed before the spring thaw restored mobility to Russia's armed forces, and before the monsoon season brought immobility to operations in southeast Asia. The Japanese timetable allowed 50 days for the capture of the Philippines, 100 days for Malaya, and 150 days for the Dutch East Indies.

While Nagumo's task force was raiding Pearl Harbor other Japanese units were taking action to prepare the way for the invasion of the Philippines. These preliminaries centred upon cutting the United States' line of communications between Hawaii and the western Pacific and upon the destruction of Lieutenant General Douglas MacArthur's Far East Air Force. Within hours of the strike against Pearl Harbor Japanese planes bombed the Islands of Guam and Wake, America's two forward outposts on the route from Hawaii to the Phillipines. On 10 December 1941 the 5,000 troops of the Japanese South Seas Detachment landed on the east and northwest shores of Guam and quickly overcame the 300 strong garrison of US Marines plus the native police. On the same day the Japanese occupied Makin and Tarawa in the British Gilbert Islands, and on 11 December a force of 500 naval landing troops accompanied by cruisers and destroyers attempted to invade Wake. The island is a tiny, completely flat atoll, but it had recently been transformed into a military base and an important air-staging post for American forces on route to the Philippines.

Wake was garrisoned by 388 men of the 1st Marine Defense Battalion supported by a Marine fighter squadron, VMF-211, with twelve Grumman F4F-3 Wildcats. It was also equipped with 5-inch coastal batteries and as the Japanese warships approached the island they were subjected to a withering barrage of gunfire. The destroyer *Hayate* was blown apart and three destroyers, a light cruiser, and a transport were damaged. The Japanese retired rapidly only to be pursued by four Wildcat fighters which sank another destroyer, damaged two cruisers, and disabled a transport. Thereafter, the Japanese bombed Wake almost daily, gradually destroying all the Wildcats and steadily draining the energy of the troops and construction workers. Unless Wake could be relieved it seemed only a matter of time before it fell to overwhelming odds.

At Pearl Harbor, Admiral Kimmel was mounting an expedition to go to the aid of Wake's defenders and all three carriers of the Pacific Fleet were committed to the operation. The *Saratoga* commanded by Admiral Frank Fletcher would deliver marines and another fighter squadron to Wake, while the *Lexington* staged a diversion by raiding Jalut in the Marshall Islands and the *Enterprise* covered Hawaii and Midway. Unfortunately, the *Saratoga* sailed towards Wake at a stately 12 knots, the maximum speed of the tanker attached to the task force. As a much reinforced Japanese invasion fleet approached the island on 22 December the *Saratoga* was still 600 miles away. Although the Japanese troops and ships at Wake would still have been vulnerable to a carrier strike the *Saratoga* and *Lexington* were recalled to Hawaii. It appeared to many that an opportunity to avenge Pearl Harbor had been missed. The Japanese had now cut the United States' line of communication across the central Pacific and the Philippines were isolated.

Exposed Allied garrisons in China also came under attack and on 8 December 1941 the Yangtze Patrol gunboat *Wake* and the United States garrison in Shanghai were captured. On 10 December the US Marines stationed at Peking and Teintsin surrendered. At 8.00 am local time on 8 December (11.30 pm, 7 December in London) the Japanese 38th Division began operations against the British garrison of the Crown Colony of Hong Kong. The Colony was a difficult place to defend. It included not only the island of Hong Kong but also a considerable part of the immediate mainland known as the Kowloon peninsula. Hong Kong was remote from other British possessions and was normally held by only four battalions of infantry and a small Royal Navy flotilla. Although there were twenty-nine coastal guns the defence lacked adequate air power and anti-aircraft artillery. Hong Kong's civilian population had been swollen by refugees from China to some one and three quarter million people and the water supply was insufficient for a prolonged siege. In August 1940, recognising the inevitable, the British Chiefs of Staff had declared that in the event of war with Japan the Colony would simply be held as an outpost for as long as possible.

In July 1941 the command of the garrison – 2nd Battalion Royal Scots, 1st Battalion Middlesex Regiment, 5th Battalion 7th Rajput, and 2nd Battalion 14th Punjab – was assumed by Major-General C M Maltby. There were also two mountain and three medium batteries of the Hong Kong and Singapore Royal Artillery, and the troops of the Hong Kong Volunteer Defence Corps. In November two Canadian Army infantry battalions, the Winnipeg Grenadiers and the Royal Rifles of Canada, arrived in the Colony

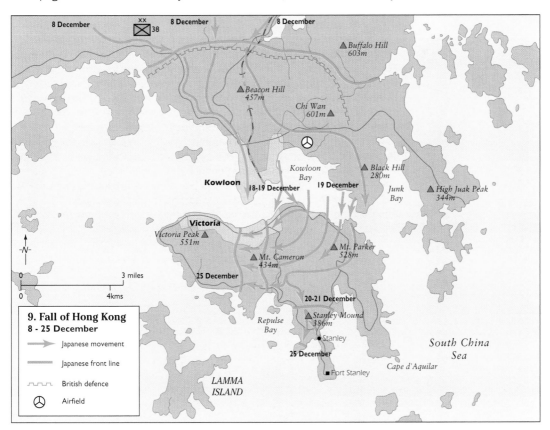

9. Fall of Hong Kong
8 - 25 December

→ Japanese movement

— Japanese front line

⌐⌐⌐ British defence

⊗ Airfield

Japanese forces parade through Hong Kong after the fall of the British colony in December 1941. The procession is headed by Lt General Sakai.

as reinforcements. The attack on Hong Kong was launched by Japanese aircraft, while three infantry regiments (228th, 229th, and 230th) supported by artillery advanced against the Colony's main defence position on the mainland, the 'Gindrinkers Line'. The Japanese gained a lodgement in the Line on the night of 9-10 December after fierce hand-to-hand fighting. The defending troops then gradually withdrew from the mainland, completing their evacuation on 13 December. The Japanese attempted to bludgeon the garrison into surrender through aerial and artillery bombardment. The fixed defence positions suffered considerable damage.

The three regiments of the 38th Division landed on Hong Kong Island on a broad front during the night of 18–19 December. By the evening of the 19th, the Japanese had occupied more than half the island. Most of the reservoirs were captured by the enemy during continued, bitter fighting, and on Christmas Day 1941 General Maltby formally surrendered his Command to Lieutenant General Sakai, of the Japanese 23rd Army. The last of the garrison laid down its arms in the early hours of 26 December. The British forces had suffered nearly 4,500 casualties during their defence of the Colony, while the Japanese lost at least 2,750 men.

With the temporary negation of American power in the Pacific the Allies could either withdraw all their naval forces from the region or fight on against impossible odds. The latter course was chosen and no clearer example of this gallant, ultimately hopeless, struggle was to be seen than in the final days of the British capital ships *Prince of Wales* and *Repulse*.

The Admiralty held many doubts concerning the deployment of the *Prince of Wales* and *Repulse* to the Far East. Churchill applied considerable pressure on the First Sea Lord, Sir Dudley Pound, and the ships designated as Force Z, finally sailed. A new aircraft carrier, HMS *Indomitable*, had been ordered to the Far East with *Prince of Wales* and *Repulse* but had been damaged by grounding off Kingston, Jamaica on 3 November 1941. On 6 December Japanese troop transports and their escorts were reported heading for the Gulf of Siam, and on the following night, 7–8 December, the enemy landed at Singora in Siam and at Kota Bahru in Malaya.

Admiral Sir Tom Phillips, Commander-in-Chief of the British Far Eastern Fleet, sailed from Singapore on the evening of 8 December with *Prince of Wales* and *Repulse*, accompanied by four destroyers. Their mission was to intercept Japanese reinforcements and bombard the enemy landings. On 9 December the force was sighted by Japanese aircraft and Admiral Phillips was informed that fighter cover could not be provided over Singora the next

The battleship HMS *Prince of Wales* coming alongside a quay in Singapore harbour on 2 December 1941. A battleship of the King George V class, the *Prince of Wales* was built between 1939 and 1941.

day. The risks of continuing with the mission were now too great and the ships reversed their course and made to return to Singapore. That night, however, a signal was received by *Prince of Wales* indicating that a Japanese landing was taking place at Kuantan. Admiral Phillips decided that since this was a critical area for the defence of Malaya, and as it was more than 400 miles from Japanese airfields in Indo-China, the *Prince of Wales* and *Repulse* should bombard the landings. In order to maintain radio silence Philips did not signal this change of plan to Singapore, but he expected that they would appreciate the significance of the landings and automatically arrange fighter protection over Kuantan the next day.

As *Prince of Wales* and *Repulse* were approaching the coast, and while Admiral Phillips was in the process of discovering that there had been no landing at Kuantan, some eighty bombers and torpedo planes from the Japanese 22nd Air Flotilla arrived overhead. Shortly after 11.00 am on 10 December the first attacks were made and *Prince of Wales* was seriously damaged by torpedoes. *Repulse* too was struck by bombs and torpedoes and by 1.20 pm both ships had capsized and sunk. Of the twin comple-ments of nearly 3,000 men serving on the *Prince of Wales* and *Repulse*, 2,081 were rescued by the destroyers, though Admiral Phillips was not among the survivors. There was now no seaworthy Allied battleship in the whole of the Pacific and Indian Oceans. The Japanese Air Force had again demonstrated both its own efficiency and the increasing obsolesence of the capital ship.

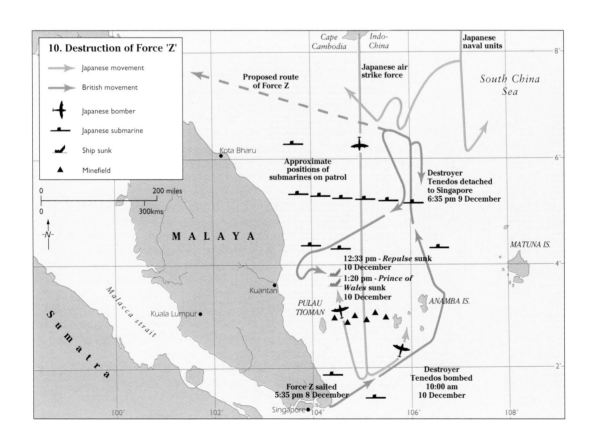

3 The Philippines, Malaya and Coral Sea

In 1924 an American author, Hector C Bywater, wrote a best-seller entitled *The Great Pacific War*. This fictional account of a war between the United States and Japan predicted a hard struggle which would begin with a series of American defeats. The five month period from the attack on Pearl Harbor to the Battle of the Coral Sea (7 December 1941–7 May 1942) amply fulfilled Bywater's prophecy as the United States and her allies in the Far East staggered from defeat to defeat. During this first phase of conquest the Japanese invaded British Borneo, Burma, Malaya, the Philippines, the Dutch East Indies and many islands throughout the western and southern Pacific. Yet bleak as the strategic picture appeared this was also a period in which the Allies could begin to glimpse eventual victory, for by its end Japan had suffered a strategic defeat and the massive potential of the United States' war effort was beginning to influence the course of events in the Pacific.

For the United States the basic strategic problem inherent in a war with Japan had always been the need to retain the use of the Philippines in the face of an enemy invasion. The planners believed that only with the Philippines available as a naval base could offensive fleet operations in the western Pacific be carried out. To lose the Philippines early in a war would damage American prestige and place in jeopardy all her interests in the Far East. Moreover, the reconquest of the islands would be a costly and lengthy undertaking involving a large commitment of naval and military resources. The problem was compounded by the fact that Japan's main naval bases were situated only some 1,500 miles from the Philippines and Japanese troops on Formosa barely 600 miles away. In contrast, Hawaii, the main base for the support of operations for the United States in the Philippines lay some 5,000 miles to the east of the islands.

The strategic plan produced to solve this problem was code named ORANGE and it was revised on a number of occasions between 1924 and 1938. United States military planners had evolved a series of outline concepts for how a war with certain nations would be conducted. Thus Plan RED dealt with war against Great Britain, Plan BLACK with Germany, Plan GREEN with Mexico, and Plan ORANGE with Japan. ORANGE took as its starting point the fact that the Philippines were regarded as the most important strategic asset for the United States in the western Pacific. Therefore the focus of offensive action by the battlefleet would be the relief of the Philippines, followed by the destruction of Japan's naval power. The garrison of the Philippines, some 17,000 troops and constabulary after World War I, was expected to hold Manila Bay until the Pacific Fleet arrived. As the fleet might take a minimum of two to three months to reach the islands, and as Japan could land upwards of 100,000 men in the first month of hostilities, it was obvious to most observers that the Philippines were very likely doomed. All the garrison could do was attempt to hold out for as long as possible and then surrender.

That the Philippines could not be successfully defended with the existing resources was clear, but neither the sponsors of Plan ORANGE – Joint Army and Navy Board – nor the politicians in Washington were prepared to admit as much to the American people. No matter how desperate the military

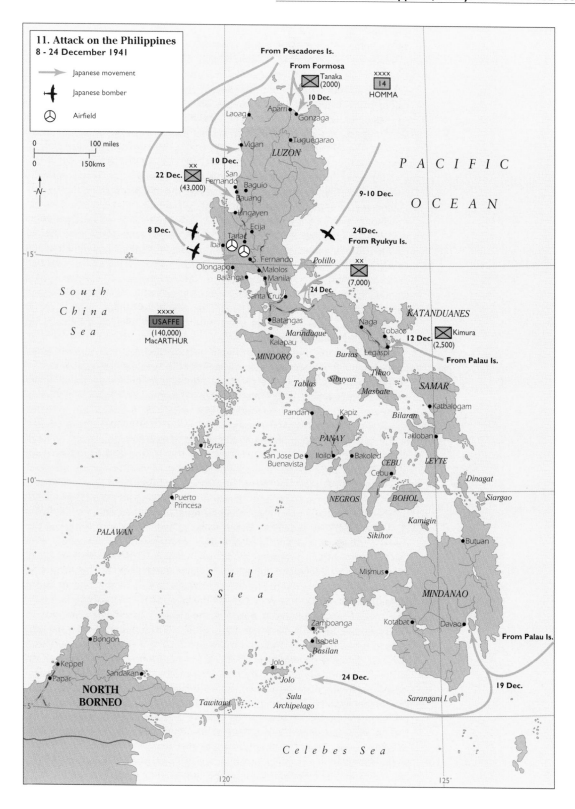

11. Attack on the Philippines
8 - 24 December 1941

→ Japanese movement

✈ Japanese bomber

Ⓜ Airfield

0 _____ 100 miles
0 _____ 150kms

-N-

From Pescadores Is.

From Formosa

Tanaka (2000)
⊠ 10 Dec.

xxxx
14
HOMMA

Laoag
Aparri
Gonzaga

Vigan
Tuguegarao

LUZON

10 Dec.
San Fernando
22 Dec. ⊠
xx
(43,000)
Baguio
Bauang
Lingayen
Ecija
9-10 Dec.

8 Dec. ✈
✈
Tarlac
Iba Ⓜ Ⓜ
24 Dec.
From Ryukyu Is.
✈

Olongapo
Balanga
S. Fernando
Malolos
Manila
Polillo
⊠ xx
(7,000)

Santa Cruz
24 Dec.

PACIFIC

OCEAN

South
China
Sea

xxxx
USAFFE
(140,000)
MacARTHUR

Batangas
Marinduque
Kalapau
MINDORO
Burias
Naga
Tobaco
Legaspi
12 Dec. ⊠
Kimura
(2,500)
From Palau Is.

KATANDUANES

Tablas
Sibuyan
Ticao
Masbate
SAMAR
Katbalogam

Pandan
Kapiz
Bilaran
Takloban

PANAY
San Jose De
Buenavista
Iloilo
Bakolod
CEBU
Cebu
LEYTE
Dinagat
Siargao

NEGROS
BOHOL

Taytay

Kamigin

Puerto
Princesa

Sikihor

Butuan

PALAWAN

Sulu
Sea

Mismus

MINDANAO

Zamboanga
Isabela
Basilan
Kotabat
Davao
From Palau Is.

Bongon

Keppel
Papar
Sandakan

Jolo
Jolo
24 Dec.
19 Dec.

NORTH
BORNEO
Tawitawi
Sulu
Archipelago
Sarangani I.

Celebes Sea

120°
125°

position, the Philippines, as the cornerstone of Pacific policy and pride, had to be held. Without Manila Bay ORANGE could not work. Throughout the interwar period, therefore, United States military policy in the Pacific was based on an offensive war carried out primarily by the navy. Revisions to ORANGE acknowledged some of the difficulties and the navy allowed that rather than a headlong dash for the Philippines it would be prudent, for example, to first establish bases along the way in the Marshalls and Carolines. It was also agreed that the garrison's task could be limited to holding the entrance to Manila Bay, using Corregidor and other close islands, rather than the entire bay area. By 1938 ORANGE set out a war plan in which offensive operations would necessarily be preceded by a defensive phase, or 'position of readiness', based upon holding the 'strategic triangle' of Alaska-Hawaii-Panama.

Despite its basic inadequacies ORANGE was in many ways a prophetic guide to how the war in the Pacific would develop, even predicting that the United States would be subject to surprise attack by Japan. Although ORANGE was never formally withdrawn it was, to some degree, superseded in October 1939, along with the other single country colour war plans, by a worldwide spectrum of five plans known collectively as RAINBOW. Each plan outlined a set of defence conditions which the United States, either alone or with a combination of allies, might have to meet in a war against Germany, Italy and Japan.

RAINBOW-1, the most basic of these plans, stipulated that United States forces, fighting without allies, would defend the Western Hemisphere north of latitude 10° south. In the Pacific a strategic defensive would be maintained from behind the line Alaska-Hawaii-Panama. RAINBOW-3, reflecting many of the conditions assumed for Plan ORANGE, provided for offensive operations into the western Pacific from Hawaii. RAINBOW-5 came closest to the actual strategy followed by the United States in World War II. In complete contrast to RAINBOW-2, which saw the United States, allied with Great Britain and France, making a major effort in the Pacific and a limited contribution in Europe, RAINBOW-5 specified that American power would be deployed against Germany and Italy as a priority. Until the Axis Powers were defeated a strategic defensive would be implemented against Japan. RAINBOW-5 enabled the greatest support to be provided for Great Britain at the earliest moment, and this approach was reinforced by the so-called 'Plan DOG' memorandum prepared by Admiral Harold R Stark, Chief of Naval Operations, for President Roosevelt in November 1940. Recognising that the security of the United States was closely linked to the fate of Great Britain, Stark swung the navy behind the 'Germany first' strategic option and away from an offensive policy in the Pacific. The major drawback to DOG was of course the fact that it gave Japan a comparatively free hand to pursue a campaign of conquest in the Far East. Similarly, the revisions to ORANGE and the development of RAINBOW had done much to confirm the isolation of the Philippines in war. By January 1941 national strategy, based on defence in the Pacific, had overturned the United States' previous reliance upon the Philippines. Once hostilities had begun there would be no naval reinforcements for the islands and the commanding officer of the Asiatic Fleet, which was based on the Philippines, was given authority to withdraw his ships to either Singapore or Hawaii.

The Philippines were now part of a secondary theatre of war but this did not mean that the United States would ignore their immediate defence. In

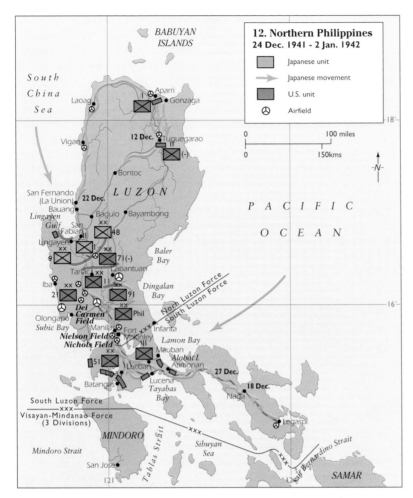

12. Northern Philippines
24 Dec. 1941 - 2 Jan. 1942

- Japanese unit
- Japanese movement
- U.S. unit
- Airfield

July 1941 the Philippine Army was embodied in the service of the United States. Lieutenant General Douglas MacArthur, the Military Adviser to the Philippine Government since 1936, was recalled from retirement to assume command of a new structure, US Army Forces in the Far East (USAFFE). MacArthur's responsibility embraced both the Philippine Army and US troops serving throughout the Philippines. Reluctant to end his career commanding the abandoned garrison of a remote Pacific outpost, MacArthur sought to convince Washington that the Philippines could be successfully defended. He argued that with the mobilisation of ten Philippine Army Divisions he would soon have nearly 200,000 men under arms. With this force, and appropriate support from Washington, the whole of the Philippines, not just Manila Bay as envisaged in Plan ORANGE, could be held. MacArthur intended to meet the invasion on the beaches where his troops would either throw the Japanese back into the sea or die in the attempt. The disquieting fact that the ten trained and equipped Philippine divisions existed only on paper, was studiously overlooked. In reality, the majority of MacArthur's troops lacked even a basic knowledge of modern war and were almost totally bereft of weapons skills, effective communications, and heavy weapons. The final factor in convincing Washington that the Philippines could be defended was the operational capability of the B-17 long range bomber, the Flying Fortress. The Army Air Corps believed that B-17s based on the Philippines could not only strike at Japanese airbases and invasion fleets but could also deter aggression over a wide area of the southwest Pacific.

An emergency reinforcement programme was underway for the Philippines by September 1941 and tanks, artillery, fighter and bomber aircraft, infantry weapons, and radar, together with additional troops, were earmarked for General MacArthur's command. An acute shortage of shipping slowed the implementation of this programme, and it was anticipated that preparations for the defence of the Philippines would not be completed before March 1942. MacArthur believed that Japan would not attack before the spring of 1942 at the earliest, and he pressed for fundamental changes in the application of RAINBOW-5 to the Philippines. Inspired by their commander's optimism the Joint Board amended the war plan on 21 November 1941, expanding the role of the garrison from the defence of Manila Bay to that of the entire Philippines. They also included orders for the planes of Far East Air Force stationed on the islands to attack any enemy forces and installations within range.

With its speed and manoeuvrability the Mitsubishi Zero had no equal as a fighter aircraft in the early years of the war and it played a crucial part in the opening Japanese campaigns.

By December 1941 the garrison of the Philippines could mount a more formidable defence than anything contemplated even six months earlier. The strength of United States ground forces, including the Philippine Scouts (Filipino troops serving in the regular United States Army), had risen to 31,000 and the Army Air Corps could put over 100 Curtiss P-40 War-hawk fighters and thirty-five B-17s into the air. The warships of the Asiatic Fleet, commanded by Admiral Thomas C Hart, had been increased to a total of three cruisers, thirteen destroyers, six gunboats, six motor torpedo boats, and twenty-nine submarines. In addition Hart could call upon thirty-two PBY Catalinas, and the men of the 4th Marine Regiment recently evac-uated from China. The Philippine divisions were still ill-equipped and under-trained but could field approximately 110,000 men.

As with the attack on Pearl Harbor, the Japanese assault upon the Philippines relied greatly upon gaining the initiative through the use of tacti-cal surprise and speed. To sustain this initiative, and ease the task of the invasion forces, it was vital that control of the air should be achieved at the earliest possible moment. As Japan's main carrier strength had been allo-cated to the raid on Hawaii, the air offensive against the Philippines was mounted principally by land-based aircraft flying from Formosa. Nearly 500 aircraft, comprising 192 planes from the 5fth Air Army Group and 304 from the 11th Air Navy Group, would prepare the way for landings by two and a half infantry divisions of the 14th Army. At sea two battleships, seven heavy cruisers, five light cruisers, and thirty-eight destroyers were available to support the invasion.

One of the basic problems faced by the Japanese in mounting the inva-sion of the Philippines was the question of providing fighter support to their bomber groups. Most army fighters had been designed for comparatively short-range operations against Siberia and their flight radius was less than 300 miles. Army bombers also lacked the range when fully loaded to attack targets in the main landing area at Lingayen Gulf, and as a result the bur-den of destroying the United States Far East Air Force would fall on navy aircraft. Yet the navy's principal fighter, the Zero, had a strike range of only some 420 miles, and the targets in Manila were 550 miles distant from the airbases on Formosa. The use of the navy's three small carriers — *Ryujo*, *Zuiho*, and *Kasuga Maru* — to close the range to the Philippines was not seen as a viable option and the only solution appeared to be to extend the Zero's combat radius. This was achieved by reducing the Zero's engine cruising speed from 1,850 revolutions per minute to 1,650–1,700 RPM, adjusting the propeller pitch, and using the leanest possible fuel mixture. With these adaptations the Zero's range was extended to 500 miles, but the precaution was taken of occupying Batan Island, 150 miles north of Luzon, on the first day of the assault. This provided a refuelling point for the Zeros on their return flight to their bases. By these relatively straightfor-ward expedients the Japanese had achieved a technological advantage which was not matched by the American P-40 fighters.

The Japanese opened their offensive against the Philippines with a strike against the bombers of the Far East Air Force based at Clark Field and the fighters at Iba. The attacking squadrons were scheduled to take off from their airfields in Formosa at 2.30 am on 8 December and to arrive over their targets shortly after dawn. This timetable involved a degree of risk since the attack would come some hours after the raid on Pearl Harbor, and the Japanese expected that the American defences in the Philippines

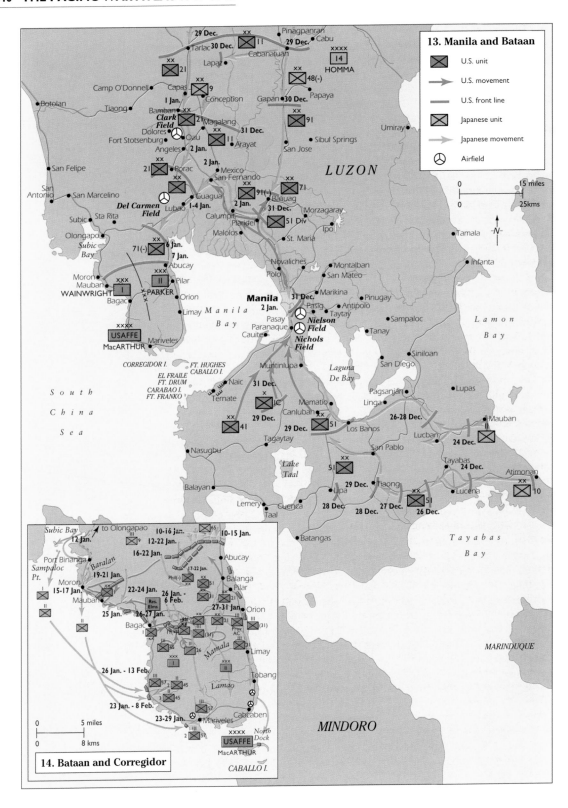

13. Manila and Bataan

- U.S. unit
- U.S. movement
- U.S. front line
- Japanese unit
- Japanese movement
- Airfield

14. Bataan and Corregidor

would be fully alert. As the time for the take-off approached, the Japanese bases on Formosa were shrouded in a dense fog and the start of the air operation was postponed. As hours of inactivity slipped by the Japanese air staff grew ever more anxious. They could not discount the possibility that American bombers were already on their way to attack the bases on Formosa, which were packed with aircraft fully fuelled and armed.

The headquarters of the Asiatic Fleet in Manila had intercepted the alert message: 'Air raid on Pearl Harbor. This is no drill' at 2.30 am on 8 December (8.00 am, 7 December in Hawaii), and by 3.30 am MacArthur and his staff were fully aware that war had finally arrived. What happened subsequently, during the nine hours which elapsed before Japanese planes arrived over their targets, is still obscure. A bomber attack on Formosa apparently suggested by General Lewis Brereton, commanding the Far East Air Force, was postponed while a photo reconnaissance flight was mounted. At about 11.00 am the bomber attack was reinstated and the B-17s, which had been airborne since 8.00 am were recalled to Clark Field to be refuelled and armed. They were still on the ground at 12.20 pm when the first Zeros, guns blazing, swept over the runway. Within an hour, fifty-four Japanese bombers and thirty-six fighters had devastated the installations at Clark Field and almost wiped out the B-17s and P-40s based there. While Clark was being put out of action, other Japanese aircraft attacked the fighter base at Iba on the west coast of Luzon, destroying all but two of the P-40s they found there.

On 9 and 10 December the Japanese continued the destruction of the Far East Air Force with raids on Nichols, Murphy, and Nielson Fields to the south of Manila and Del Carmen to the northwest. The bombers also turned their attention to the shipping in Manila Bay and to Cavite Naval Base, though most of the Asiatic Fleet with the exception of its submarines, had already sailed south out of range. Exactly where the responsibility for these disasters lay was clouded by a welter of recrimination and denial between MacArthur, his Chief of Staff General Richard Sutherland, and Brereton. Certainly the Japanese could hardly believe their good fortune for in two days, and with only minimal losses they had all but destroyed United States air power in the Philippines and the Far East.

Although Japanese landings in the Philippines – at Aparri, Davao, Legaspi, and Vigan – had taken place while the air attack was in progress, these were expeditions with the specific purpose of capturing advance airfields, cutting communications between Manila and the south, and securing bases for the assault on Borneo. They were successful precursors to the main invasion by the 14th Army which took place at Lingayen Gulf 120 miles to the north of Manila on 22 December 1941. Troops of Lieutenant General Homma Masaharu's two divisions – the 16th and 48th – were opposed by two Philippine Army divisions supported by the Philippine Scouts of the 26th Cavalry. None of the Philippine units were fully equipped and they were forced to fall back as the Japanese advanced on Baguio, the Philippine summer capital.

With the destruction of a large part of the Far East Air Force and the transfer of the surviving B-17s to Australia, the only American units capable of disputing Japanese control of the waters around the Philippines were the twenty-nine submarines of the Asiatic Fleet. There were, however, a number of factors working against their effectiveness. In the comparatively shallow coastal waters off the northern Philippines submarines were easily spotted from the air, even when submerged, and when depth-charged there was little room for them to manoeuvre. When they attacked Japanese shipping their new Mark XIV steam torpedoes often malfunctioned. Two enemy ships were sunk as a result of sixty-six torpedoes fired.

On 24 December MacArthur put Plan ORANGE into operation, declaring Manila an open city and evacuating the government and his headquarters to the island fortress of Corregidor at the mouth of Manila Bay. MacArthur also gave orders for a general retreat to the Bataan Peninsula, and on the same day 7,000 Japanese troops landed in Lamon Bay as part of the envelopment of the capital from north and south. The United States and Philippine troops now undertook a two week fighting withdrawal into Bataan, delaying the Japanese at successive defensive positions designated D-1 to D-5. This provided time for a proportion of the supplies dispersed across Luzon to be assembled in the peninsula, and for the withdrawal of Brigadier General Albert Jones' South Luzon Force from the Lamon Bay area.

The Japanese occupied Manila on 2 January 1942 but they were unable to use the port while MacArthur held Corregidor and Bataan. There were also undefeated American and Philippine troops on Bohol, Cebu, Leyte, Mindanao, Panay and other islands, and before General Homma could begin his assault on Bataan the 14th Army was seriously weakened by the transfer of the 48th Division to another operation. As reinforcements Homma received the 65th Brigade, but he considered this unit unfit for combat due to lack of training and experience. Nevertheless he expected little serious resistance from the American and Philippine defenders and he entrusted what he believed would be largely a mopping-up operation to the 65th Brigade. In fact, the Brigade found itself opposed by an American defence line running across the peninsula, from Mauban in the west to Mabating on Manila Bay. In all there were now some 90,000 troops defending Bataan with those in the main defence line organised in two corps under, in the west, Major General Jonathan Wainwright and, in the east, Major General George Parker. Wainwright's corps comprised three Philippine Army Divisions (1st, 31st, and 91st) and the 26th Cavalry, while Parker commanded four Philippine Army Divisions (11th, 21st, 41st, and 51st) plus a Philippine Scout regiment, the 57th.

The American position in Bataan suffered from a number of serious weaknesses. The defenders, although outnumbering the Japanese, were already on half-rations, were short of medical supplies, and were increasingly debilitated by beriberi, dysentery and malaria. They also eventually lost hope, for despite MacArthur's impassioned pleas to Washington for reinforcement it became clear that the Philippines could expect no support, short of what could be run through the blockade by submarine. At the front communications were inadequate, and the main defence line across the peninsula was poorly fortified and split into two separate zones by Mount Natib, over 4,000 feet high. Even so, when the Japanese opened their attack on 9 January they were held for six days until a breakthrough in the 51st Division's sector, east of Mount Natib, threatened to outflank Parker. Counterattacks failed to dislodge the enemy, and by 21 January Wainwright was also in danger of envelopment as the Japanese crossed the reputedly impassable heights of Natib and established a road block behind his position. On 24 January MacArthur ordered a general withdrawal to a second defence line, eight miles to the south, spanning the peninsula between

Bagac in the west and Orion in the east. He expected there to be no further retreat from this line:

'With its occupation all manoeuvring possibilities will cease. I intend to fight it out to complete destruction.'

The troops on both sides were close to exhaustion and the Japanese 65th Brigade had suffered nearly 25 per cent casualties. Nevertheless, Homma launched a series of frontal attacks by the 16th Division together with three amphibious landings along the southwest corner of the peninsula behind the American defences. Both the landings and a penetration of Wainwright's positions were eventually destroyed, and Homma, his casualties mounting and his remaining troops racked by sickness, was forced to call a halt and request reinforcements. For almost two months from 8

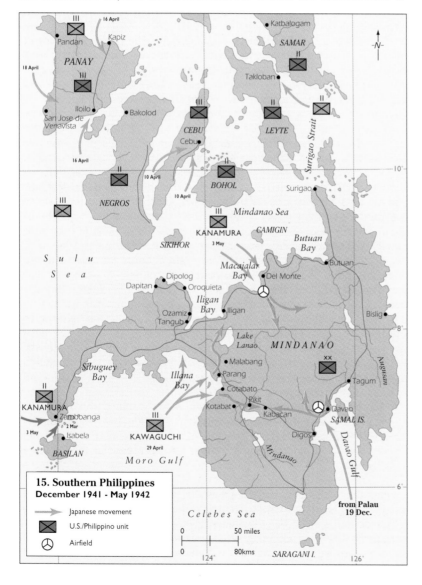

15. Southern Philippines
December 1941 - May 1942

→ Japanese movement

⊠ U.S./Philippino unit

⊗ Airfield

February to 3 April 1942 the Japanese laid siege to Bataan. On 22 February Roosevelt ordered MacArthur to leave the Philippines for Australia to assume command of a new southwest Pacific theatre. At first MacArthur refused to go, only relenting after discussions with his staff and with an agreement that he could choose the appropriate moment. On 11 March, pledging to return one day, MacArthur left via PT boat for Australia via Mindanao. General Wainwright assumed command in the Philippines in his absence.

While the strength of the defenders ebbed even further – the daily ration for the troops on Bataan had been reduced to a mere 1,000 calories a day by late March – General Homma's command was reinforced by a fresh division (14th), by parts of a second (21st), and by powerful artillery and air units. At the beginning of April the Japanese attacked and the defence, now in a pitiful condition with men almost too weak to aim their rifles, collapsed. The commanding officer on Luzon, Major General Edward King, ignored a totally unrealistic order from MacArthur to mount a general counterattack and surrendered his force on 9 April. The heroic survivors of Bataan were thereafter subjected by the Japanese to the atrocities and humiliations of the Death March into captivity.

Although General Homma now controlled all of Luzon, he was still denied the use of Manila harbour by the continued resistance of Corregidor and its outlying forts in the entrance to the bay. Corregidor was an island fortress but its strong defences were designed to repel an attack from the sea not from the land. For nearly four weeks, from 9 April to 6 May, the Japanese shelled and bombed Corregidor remorselessly. Even though the 10,000 strong garrison could secure some shelter underground in the Malinta Tunnel, conditions quickly became intolerable as water, food and ammunition supplies steadily dwindled. By the beginning of May the defenders, their artillery emplacements destroyed, their communications smashed or blown into the sea, and their defences wrecked, could offer little hope of further resistance. Yet when the Japanese landed on the eastern end of the island on the night of 5–6 May they met a withering fire which inflicted heavy casualties. As the battle for the island continued through the night and into the next morning the defence was gradually worn down and the appearance of three enemy tanks came as the last straw. With his casualties rapidly mounting and with the Japanese now close to the entrance of the Malinta Tunnel and the 1,000 wounded housed there, General Wainwright had to surrender or risk a massacre. At midday on 6 May 1942 the American flag on Corregidor was lowered. In a moving and dignified last message to the President, General Wainwright wrote:

'With broken heart and head bowed in sadness but not in shame I report ... that today I must arrange terms for the surrender of the fortified islands of Manila Bay. ...With profound regret and with continued pride in my gallant troops, I go to meet the Japanese commander.'

While the Japanese were attempting to smash Corregidor their troops were landing on the Visayan Islands in the central Philippines and on Mindanao to the south, but there were several islands where American garrisons still held out. Accordingly the Japanese insisted that Wainwright's surrender applied to the whole of the Archipelago. Organised resistance on the Philippines thus came to an end, but many Filipino and some American troops took to the mountains to wage guerrilla war rather than become prisoners. In taking the Philippines the Japanese had suffered approximately 12,000 casualties; American and Philippine units some 16,000 plus 84,000 prisoners of war. It was a bitter defeat.

Strategically the defence of the Philippines was not of great significance. It did not seriously hamper Japanese operations elsewhere and it did not cause Great Britain and the United States to alter their policy of assigning priority to the war in Europe. Tactically and psychologically, however, the defenders of the Philippines had made a telling point. Only in the Philippines had the Japanese offensive looked in danger of stalling, and only on the battlefields of Bataan had the dominance of their troops appeared fragile.

MacArthur's conduct of the defence of the Philippines was tactically flawed and showed serious errors of leadership. Despite warnings of what was happening at Pearl Harbor, MacArthur allowed the bulk of his airforce to be destroyed on the ground. His decision to disperse his troops and their supplies in an attempt to defend the entire Archipelago, rather than withdrawing to Bataan as soon as the Japanese landed, seriously compromised the defence and resulted in appalling suffering among his troops who were denied ammunition, adequate food and medical supplies. MacArthur's remoteness, egotism, self-aggrandisement, and distortions of reality alienated his naval commander, Admiral Hart, and jeopardised the morale of his troops. Yet instead of immediate relief from his command, MacArthur became a national hero, the recipient of the Medal of Honor, and the object of adulation by all except the starved and disease-ridden men on Bataan and Corregidor. His opponent, General Homma, ultimately successful, though in five months rather than two, had lost face and was relieved of his command.

American prisoners of war, the survivors of Bataan, forming part of the Death March into captivity after the surrender of US forces in Luzon to the Japanese in April 1942. Thousands of Americans died from disease, malnutrition and ill-treatment by their captors on this notorious march.

While the defenders of the Philippines had been fighting their isolated battle, the implications of Japanese success elsewhere were being assessed in Washington and London. The apparent destruction of the offensive power of the Pacific Fleet at Pearl Harbor led to radical modifications of RAINBOW-5. The task of the Pacific Fleet was now almost entirely defensive and plans to take the Marshal and Caroline Islands and to help Great Britain defend Malaya were deleted. Instead of the transfer of warships from the Pacific to the Mediterranean to enable the British to reinforce their fleet in the Far East, the carrier *Yorktown*, three battleships, twelve submarines, and nine destroyers left the Atlantic for service in the Pacific. The seemingly inexorable Japanese advance across the Pacific and southeast Asia placed Roosevelt under enormous pressure to rejuvenate the United States command in the Pacific. General Short and Admiral Kimmel were removed from their posts and within weeks both had been retired from the armed service. The new Commander-in-Chief of the Pacific Fleet was Admiral Chester W Nimitz, then Chief of the Bureau of Navigation. Nimitz had graduated from the Naval Academy in 1905 and served on a wide range of warships, becoming captain of a submarine and an expert on diesel engines. Although not an officer for whom audacity and innovation were priorities, Nimitz was well versed in the problems of fighting a war against the Japanese in the Pacific. He had studied at the Naval War College where a constant theme was the refinement of Plan ORANGE through wargames and chart exercises. Nimitz and his contemporaries from the Academy were to run the Pacific War along lines that had largely been determined before a shot was fired. As Nimitz later remarked:

'The course (at the Naval War College) was so complete that when war in the Pacific actually started, nothing that happened surprised us at all except the Kamikaze attacks.'

General Short's replacement was Lieutenant General Delos C. Emmons, while the air commander in Hawaii, Major General Frederick Martin was superseded by Brigadier General Clarence L Tinker. General Marshal, Chief of Staff United States Army, survived the opening disasters of the war but Admiral Stark, who had temporarily lost Roosevelt's favour, was eventually reassigned to the European theatre, allowing Admiral Ernest J King to be appointed both Commander-in-Chief of the US Fleet and Chief of Naval Operations. During the ARCADIA Conference held between President Roosevelt, Prime Minister Churchill and their military Staffs in Washington (22 December 1941–14 January 1942), the president converted the Joint Army-Navy Board into the Joint Chiefs of Staff. When the Joint Chiefs met their British counterparts, the Chiefs of Staff Committee, in conference they were collectively titled the Combined Chiefs of Staff.

An immediate problem facing the Combined Chiefs of Staff was the establishment of an effective command structure in the Far East. At the ARCADIA Conference General Marshall pressed for a unified command under a Supreme Commander. The proposal was backed by Roosevelt but initially opposed by Churchill and Admiral King, and there was considerable disagreement as to whether the Supreme Commander should be American or British. The eventual solution was the creation of a joint American, British, Dutch, Australian Command (ABDACOM) under a British Army officer, General Sir Archibald Wavell.

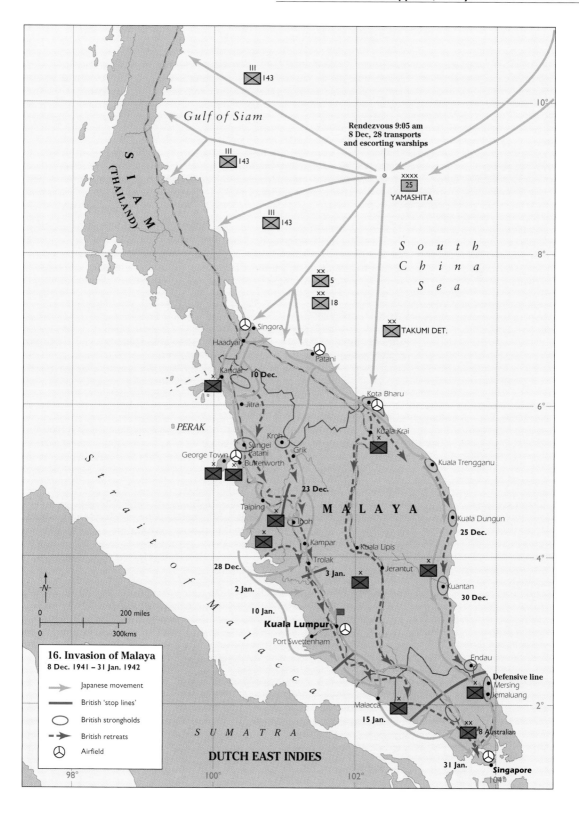

Marshall had wanted unity of command covering all naval, ground and air forces in the Far East, but Wavell's authority stopped short of this. He was Supreme Commander of all theatres of war in the Far East except for China, Indo-China, Siam, Australia south of Darwin, and the majority of the Pacific. In broad terms Wavell's command, which was designated as the Southwest Pacific Area, included the Andaman and Nicobar Islands, Burma, the Christmas and Cocos Islands, Malaya, the Netherlands East Indies, and the Philippines. Wavell assumed responsibility for this area on 15 January 1942 and from the start he was beset by problems at a number of critical points, not least in Malaya.

The Japanese had launched their invasion of Malaya some thirty minutes before the attack on Pearl Harbor with a landing at Kota Bharu on the northeast coast of the peninsula in the early hours of 8 December 1941. This was quickly followed by the main landings at Patani and Singora in Siam and by landings at the neck of the Kra Isthmus and at Bangkok. These operations were assigned to two Japanese armies. The 15th Army, consisting of two divisions (33rd and 55th less one infantry regiment) was supported by the 10th Air Brigade (from 3rd Air Division) and by the temporary attachment of the Imperial Guards Division. Its task was the occupation of Siam and, eventually, an advance into southern Burma to cut land communications between India and Malaya and to capture Rangoon. The 25fth Army comprising four divisions was to secure a lodgement in northern Malaya before advancing south to take Singapore.

The focal point of British military power in Malaya and the Far East was the naval base at Singapore, and in the eyes of many its defence ranked second in importance only to that of the United Kingdom. Singapore's strategic role was founded on the belief that, in war, it would be secured by the arrival of a Royal Navy battlefleet from European waters. During the late 1930s it began to appear that this policy was increasingly untenable if Great Britain should find herself engaged in war both in the Far East and in Europe. Accordingly, in August 1940, the burden of Malaya's defence was switched to the Royal Air Force whose planes, distributed across the Peninsula, would in theory sink an invasion fleet before it reached land. The Army's task would be to defend key installations and the airfields from which the RAF's planned strength of twenty-two squadrons and 336 aircraft would operate. It was estimated that some ten brigades, reducing eventually to six, would be necessary for this role. However, by December 1941 only thirteen squadrons with 158 front-line aircraft, many of those of obsolete types, were available in Malaya. The Army could field ten brigades organised as three divisions and one independent brigade, but individual units lacked heavy weapons, and particularly tanks and artillery.

To achieve the range required to strike at the enemy over the Gulf of Siam and at his bases in southern Indo-China, the RAF's airfields had been built well forward in eastern and northern Malaya. This produced a difficult problem for the army, which would have to defend parts of the east coast of Malaya, and a strip of territory running north along the frontier with Siam, which would have been best abandoned. They could not be, however, since they contained groups of airfields at Kota Bharu, Kuantan, Alor Star and Sungei Patani. As a result, a substantial part of the army's ten brigades would be isolated from the rest of the defence force and would thus be natural targets for envelopment. In an attempt to reconcile these contradictions it was proposed that the best form of defence for northern Malaya might be an advance into Siam itself. This plan, which was known by the code word MATADOR, would forestall an enemy attack by forming a shorter and better defence line across the neck of the Kra Isthmus, and by seizing the aerodrome and Port of Singora. The difficulty was in choosing the correct moment to advance over 100 miles into neutral Siam. The defence of Singapore was thrown into further confusion by the Japanese occupation of southern Indo-China, for at a stroke the enemy had gained the ideal springboard for an attack on Siam, Burma and Malaya. The General Officer Commanding in Malaya, Lieutenant General A E Percival, revised his defence needs in the light of this development. He estimated that safeguarding Malaya would now require a minimum of five infantry divisions plus artillery and armoured units. Yet little help could be spared either in men or equipment. Great Britain was already defending India and the United Kingdom, fighting a campaign against the Germans and Italians in north Africa, and sending aid to Russia.

Although air reconnaissance sighted two or three Japanese convoys sailing west and northwest from Indo-China during 6 December 1941, the northeast monsoon made observation difficult and the convoys were not located again until the evening of 7 December. In the absence of definite pointers as to the destination of these convoys MATADOR was not put into operation. When the Japanese land at Kota Bharu on 8 December, the British assumed that this was their principal point of attack and the main RAF strength was directed against it. The Japanese suffered heavy casual-

Japanese troops in mopping-up operations in Kuala Lumpur during the invasion of Malaya.

ties but this concentration of effort meant that the Japanese landings at Patani and Singora in Siam went ahead unhindered. Troops from the 55th Division landed at the neck of the Kra Isthmus and part of the Imperial Guards Division at Bangkok. In addition an overland invasion took place across the Indo-Chinese frontier and squadrons of the 3rd Air Division moved forward to occupy airfields in Siam.

The Japanese 5th Division, supported by tanks, launched attacks down the east and west coasts of Malaya, forcing the British from defended positions in the east by infiltration through the jungle, and in the west by amphibious hooks along the coast. The 11th Indian Division, caught between the need to fight delaying actions while at the same time preparing new defensive positions, was defeated on the Slim River on 7 January 1942. The defence of Northern Johore now became impossible, although troops of the 8th Australian Division under Major General H Gordon Bennett inflicted a timely defeat on the Japanese at Gemas on 14 January. Reinforcements were arriving at Singapore, amongst them the 44th and 45th Indian Brigades, the 53rd British Brigade and the 18th British Division, but the speed of the Japanese advance meant that they were thrown into battle piecemeal and largely unprepared. The Japanese were engaged and held at Parit Sulong and Pelandok between 20–23 January, but the capture of Endau on the east coast of the peninsula meant that effectively Johore was already lost.

By 31 January the mainland had been evacuated and the causeway between Johore Bahru and Singapore Island destroyed. The British command hoped that Singapore would be able to hold out for some months, and that it would eventually provide a launch point for a counter-offensive, but its defences were designed to repel an attack from the sea not from across the Johore Strait. As the island extended for only some twenty-seven miles from east to west and thirteen miles from north to south, a number of vital installations and airfields were within artillery range of the mainland. With the decision to transfer all but a token number of fighters to Sumatra enemy air raids became almost continuous, and conditions rapidly worsened for both the civilian population of nearly one million and the 85,000 defending troops. In the garrison General Percival could call upon seventeen Indian, thirteen British, six Australian, and two Malay infantry battalions, plus one reconnaissance and three machine gun battalions. There were also three Volunteer battalions, four airfield defence battalions and supporting artillery units. The appearance of strength in depth was a sham, however, for many units in the garrison were under establishment, poorly equipped and only partly trained. Several had only recently arrived in Singapore after a debilitating three month sea voyage, and others were short of officers, composed of young recruits, or totally lacking in experience of active service. By deploying the garrison around the whole island in an attempt to defend seventy miles of coastline, and with only one brigade held in reserve, Percival risked his troops being defeated in detail. The coordination of this static defence once the Japanese had landed became an increasingly difficult task.

The main Japanese assault on Singapore was carried out by sixteen battalions of the 5th and 18th Divisions on the night of 8–9 February. It struck the west coast of the island between Tanjong Buloh and Tanjong Murai and met determined opposition, with some landings only succeeding at the second or third attempt. Once ashore, the strength of the Japanese attack

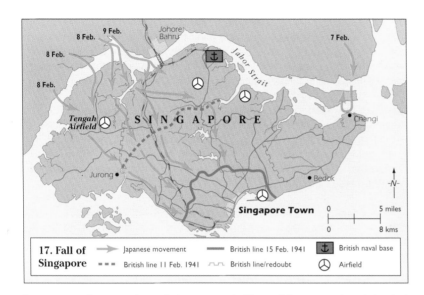

17. Fall of Singinpore

→ Japanese movement	━━ British line 15 Feb. 1941
▪▪▪ British line 11 Feb. 1941	⌐⌐ British line/redoubt
⚓ British naval base	
⊗ Airfield	

began to tell as parties of the enemy infiltrated between the defended localities and attacked individual units from all sides. The defence was saturated by sheer weight of numbers. On the evening of 9 February elements of the Japanese Imperial Guards Division launched an assault immediately to the west of the Causeway. At first they made little progress against the 27th Australian Brigade and only as more and more landing craft put troops ashore did the Australians, now seriously reduced in number, fall back. As the Japanese pushed out across the island they met stiff resistance, but they were able to deploy tanks in overwhelming force to support their attacks, At one point during the night of 10–11 February, troops of the 2nd Battalion the Argyll and Sutherland Highlanders found themselves opposed by fifty Japanese tanks near Bukit Timah. By 11 February the Japanese had secured the western part of Singapore and it was now only a question of time before they overran the whole island. Gradually the defenders were pressed back in all sectors and General Percival ordered a twenty-eight mile defence perimeter to be formed around Singapore town itself. By 13 February the garrison had withdrawn into this line, but on the next day the Japanese broke through in the western outskirts of Singapore and General Percival surrendered his command on 15 February 1942. As a result of the battle for Malaya 130,000 British and Commonwealth troops became prisoners of war.

In a campaign lasting just seventy days the Japanese had driven the British out of Malaya and had captured their main strategic fortress in the Far East. Wavell's Chief of Staff, General Sir Henry Pownall, writing on 13 February echoed the thoughts of many throughout Great Britain and the Commonwealth:

'It is a great disaster for British Arms, one of the worst in history, and a great blow to the honour and prestige of the Army. From the beginning to the end of this campaign we have been outmatched by better soldiers.'

The Japanese troops used in Malaya had been trained in jungle warfare

Lieutenant General Arthur Percival surrenders Singapore to the Japanese on 15 February 1942.

and many had experience of combat in China. They were tough, expert soldiers who were well led and who were used to taking risks. The bravery and sacrifice of individual British and Commonwealth soldiers could not redress the disadvantages under which they fought. General Wavell identified the principal problems in a note dated 17 February 1942:

'The trouble goes a long way back; climate, the atmosphere of the country (the whole of Malaya has been asleep for at least two hundred years), lack of vigour in our peacetime training, the cumbersomeness of our tactics and equipment, and the real difficulty of finding an answer to the very skilful and bold tactics of the Japanese in this jungle fighting.'

With its Malayan flank now secure the Japanese 15th Army (33rd and 55th Divisions) was free to develop the operations it had already begun in Burma.

The geography of Burma presented a serious obstacle to military operations. In 1941, in a country covering 240,000 square miles or approximately three times the size of Great Britain, there was not a single through road and the tracks which did exist were liable to disruption by monsoon floods and landslides. The interior was surrounded on three sides by formidable mountain ranges and on the fourth by the sea, with at first only a few difficult trails linking Burma to Siam and India. The jungle covered hills, which ran with monotonous regularity across much of the country, were intersected by fast rivers plunging through deep sided valleys. The only port capable of supplying an army was at Rangoon and the only effective form of inland transport was by river. Movement on any scale became almost impossible during the southwest monsoon which lasted from mid-May to mid-October, while the northeast monsoon occupied the months from November to February. In between, in April and May, temperatures soared to over 100° Fahrenheit and thunderstorms were a regular occurrence. In addition to exceptionally heavy rainfall which swept away tracks and bridges, the monsoons ensured that troops fought soaked to the skin and with their equipment rotting as they carried it. In Burma disease and infection flourished. Cholera, smallpox, scrub typhus, malaria and dysentery were endemic, and at times they became almost more intractable opponents than the Japanese.

The British had annexed Burma in the course of three wars – in 1824, 1852, and 1885 – fought largely to ensure that the eastern frontier of India

Soldiers of the King's own Royal Regiment (Lancaster) together with a platoon of Indian troops on parade at Rangoon's Sale Barracks in Burma in 1924.

Japanese soldiers taking part in a victory cheer in front of the former headquarters of the British Governor General of Burma after the capture of Rangoon.

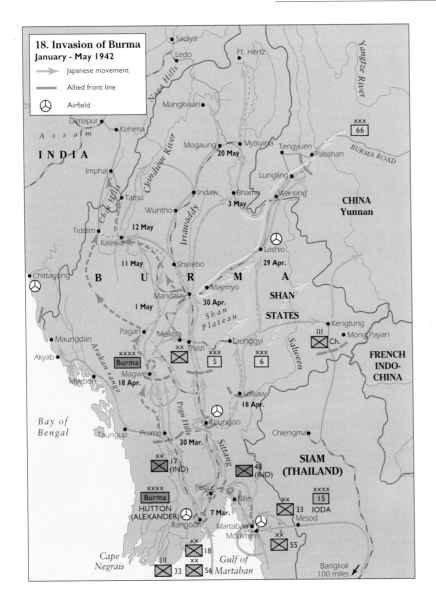

18. Invasion of Burma
January - May 1942

→ Japanese movement

━━ Allied front line

Ⓐ Airfield

remained tranquil. By 1941 Burma had achieved considerable strategic importance. It protected the industrial centres of northeast India from air attack and it provided the only route, from Rangoon to Mandalay and along the Burma Road, by which war supplies could be transported to the Chinese and to the American air squadrons operating in China. For the Japanese the occupation of Burma would protect the northwest flank of the Greater East Asian Co-Prosperity Sphere, and provide a further source of rice and oil. The garrison of Burma was normally no more than two battalions of British infantry, supported by locally enlisted units and military police, but as the situation in the Far East deteriorated during 1941 an expansion of the local Burmese forces was set in motion, and reinforcements were sent from India. By the beginning of 1942 Lieutenant General Sir Thomas Hutton, commanding in Burma, could deploy, on paper, the best part of two divisions, the 1st Burma and 17th Indian. Neither division, however, was fully equipped or trained and the 1st Burma Division lacked supporting services and artillery. Hutton's air power was limited and during the campaign he was able to call upon only some nine and a half squadrons, including one from the American Volunteer Group (AVG). The Chinese 5th and 6th Armies, under the nominal command of Major General Joseph ('Vinegar Joe') Stilwell, were offered by Chiang Kai-shek to support British operations in Burma providing certain conditions as to their deployment could be met.

In December 1941 the Japanese had crossed the border from Siam into Burma and had occupied Victoria Point on the west of the Kra Isthmus. In January 1942 they launched a campaign which placed the security of Rangoon and indeed the whole British position in Burma in jeopardy. On 15 January, Japanese troops advanced from Siam towards Moulmein on the east bank of the Salween River and quickly captured all three airfields on the Tenasserim coast. They were now in a position to provide fighter escort for their bombing raids on Rangoon, an important consideration as their attacks were tenaciously opposed by the outnumbered squadrons of the Royal Air Force and the AVG. The British response concentrated on the defence of south Burma in the hope that the advance of the 15th Army could be held until reinforcements arrived through Rangoon. The difficulty of using Rangoon as a base, since it was vulnerable to air, land and sea attack, was obvious, however, and Hutton took the precaution of backloading stores to depots in upper Burma. The covering force for Rangoon was provided by the 17th Indian Division, commanded by Major General J G Smyth VC, and the 2nd Burma Brigade. Their primary task was to hold the Japanese to the east of the Salween River. The 1st Burma Division, now with only two brigades, was given responsibility for the defence of the Shan States in central Burma.

A familiar picture began to appear as the advancing Japanese troops threatened Allied units with encirclement, thereby causing them to fall back in confusion. By 11 February Japanese attacks in the north had created a bridgehead west of the Salween. Threatened by envelopment, the 17th Indian Division began a retreat to the line of the Bilin River on 14 February. This was a weak, dispersed position which some Japanese units reached before the defending troops, and on 18 February Smyth was authorised to withdraw to the River Sittang, the last major defence line before Rangoon. The withdrawal turned into a disaster for although the Headquarters of the 17th Indian Division successfully crossed to the west bank of the river, the single bridge was blown up with a large part of the division still on the east bank. Under attack from enemy troops and aircraft many units attempted to cross the river by rafts or swimming, but casualties were considerable.

Rangoon was now exposed and General Hutton was inclined to order its evacuation. This was countermanded by Wavell since reinforcements in the form of the 7th Armoured Brigade and the 63rd Indian Infantry Brigade were then at sea on route to Rangoon. At the beginning of March Wavell, finding General Smyth in poor health, placed Brigadier D T Cowan in command of 17th Indian Division, and on 5 March Lieutenant General the Honourable Sir Harold Alexander replaced General Hutton in command in Burma. Alexander's instructions were to hold Rangoon for as long as possible and then to withdraw northwards to prepare for the defence of upper Burma. There he was to stabilise the front in order to maintain contact with the

Chinese, secure the oil fields at Yenangyaung, and cover the construction of the road from Assam into Burma.

Alexander was given little time in which to consider his orders, for by 5 March the Japanese had already crossed the Sittang and Pegu rivers, and were making for the Irrawaddy. There was a very real danger that the British and Indian troops covering Rangoon would be cut off, and on 6 March Alexander ordered a withdrawal to the north. With the 7th Armoured Brigade and the 17th Indian Division mounting a flank and rearguard, the British just managed to slip by the Japanese 33rd Division as it crossed the axis of their retreat to Prome. Rangoon and Southern Burma were lost and the Japanese, already close to exhausting their supplies on more than one occasion, had gained a port that could transform their logistics. The British, in contrast, now had to march into the centre of Burma without a line of communication or base, withdrawing all the time towards India.

With the fall of Rangoon and the improvement in their supply position the Japanese deployed two new divisions, the 18th and 56th to advance north, supported by armoured units, along the valleys of the Sittang and Irrawaddy rivers. Alexander requested that the 5th and 6th Chinese Armies cover his eastern flank at Toungoo and in the Shan States while he attempted to hold the Japanese around Prome. The British deployed the 17th Indian Division, 7th Armoured Brigade, 1st Burma Division and supporting troops, as Burcorps under the command of Lieutenant General W J 'Bill' Slim. The Chinese held out at Toungoo until 30 March, and attempts by Slim's troops to relieve the pressure on them by a limited counteroffensive served only to weaken the British defence at Prome. With the capture of Toungoo the entire Allied position was threatened from the east, and it was only a question of time before the whole of Burma was lost. Burcorps was by now sadly depleted in strength and its remaining troops were already weak from disease and thirst. As they retreated northwards they were subjected to deadly attacks from the air, constant infiltration by Japanese ground troops, and a perilous supply position. Yet under Slim's inspirational leadership they repeatedly hit back at the advancing enemy, teaching the Japanese a healthy respect for Burcorp's rearguards. As the enemy closed in on Mandalay the British and Chinese armies diverged to follow their own routes in retreat, the British via the Myittha and Chindwin valleys to Kalewa and Imphal, the Chinese eastwards into Yunnan and north to Assam.

On 20 May 1942, as the Allied forces withdrew across the River Chindwin, the battle for Burma, five and a half months in duration, came to an end. In the longest retreat in its history, the British Army had carried out a 1,000 mile fighting withdrawal through some of the worst terrain and conditions in the world. Many lessons had been learned during the retreat and they would be applied during the successful campaign to retake Burma. It was, however, another defeat characterised by British unpreparedness, by troops partly or wrongly trained, and by confusion in command. China was now isolated and to keep her in the war the Allies were forced to devote considerable effort to the maintenance of an air route, and to the opening of a land route. As General Stilwell remarked on his return to India:

> 'I claim we got a hell of a beating. We got run out of Burma and it is humiliating as hell. I think we ought to find out what caused it, go back and retake it.'

While the invasions of Burma, Malaya and the Philippines were in progress the Japanese were also carrying out operations against the strategically important chain of islands forming part of the Malay barrier. The barrier, which was flanked by Burma in the west and Australia in the east comprised the Malay Peninsula, Sumatra, Java, and the Dutch islands running eastwards to New Guinea. The sheer expanse of the Dutch East Indies and the multiplicity of islands from which they were formed made their defence extremely difficult. The main Dutch forces, supplemented at critical points by other Allied units, particularly British, Indian, and Australian, were concentrated in Java. As a result the forward bases in Borneo and Celebes could only be lightly held. The Dutch had constructed modern airfields but few of the Allies modern planes survived long enough to make full use of them, and the lack of adequate roads on the larger islands reduced the flexibility of the defence. When the Japanese gained a beachhead they brought in land based aircraft to operate from captured airfields, eliminated the local garrison, and leapfrogged forward to their next objective. The Japanese assault on British Borneo provides an example of the tempo of these operations and an indication of the predicament of isolated garrisons suddenly faced by strong landing parties.

The island of Borneo was partly Dutch and partly British, with the British section comprising British North Borneo, Sarawak, the State of Brunei, and Labuan Island. Borneo lies across the main sea routes from the south Pacific to Malaya, Sumatra, Java, Celebes, and the Indian Ocean. It thus had considerable strategic importance, and was also a source of oil and raw materials, but neither the British nor the Dutch had sufficient forces to defend Borneo against a serious assault. The British in fact decided that only Kuching in western Sarawak would be defended and the 2nd Battalion 15th Punjab Regiment was dispatched there in May 1941. The Japanese 35th Infantry Brigade Headquarters, the Yokosuka 2nd Special Naval Landing Force, and the 124th Infantry Regiment (3 battalions with approximately 2,600 men), landed in Sarawak on 15 December and then proceeded to occupy British North Borneo and Brunei. They reached Kuching on 24 December and fought a furious action with the Punjabis from the beach to the airfield perimeter. During the morning of 25 December the Japanese attempted to work round the airfield defences and at about noon the commanding officer of the Punjabis, Lieutenant Colonel C M Lane, ordered a withdrawal into Dutch Borneo. The Japanese, quickly realising what was happening, mounted an immediate all-out attack on the two companies of Punjabis forming the rearguard. Only one platoon escaped and the remainder, 230 men and four officers, were either killed or captured. On 29 December the rest of the Battalion reached the Singkawang II airfield in Dutch Borneo and Colonel Lane placed his men under Dutch command. The Punjabis were in action against the Japanese on 26 and 27 December, and two Punjabi platoons which became surrounded fought on until they had exhausted their ammunition and then surrendered. It has been estimated that the Punjabis inflicted between 400–500 casualties on the enemy. The Japanese took instant revenge for only three men from the seventy soldiers comprising these platoons were ever seen again. Having fought a number of rearguard actions, the survivors of the Battalion divided into two columns and made for the south coast of Dutch Borneo in the hope of finding a ship or local boats to Java. They were not successful and after ten weeks in action and a march of some 800 miles through appalling country the Punjabi troops finally surrendered on 9 March 1942.

Landings in Dutch Borneo began at Tarakan on 10 January 1942 and Balikpapan on Christmas Eve, and these were followed by a cross border invasion by Japanese troops from Sarawak and a land assault on Bandjermasin. Celebes was occupied between 11 January and 8 February 1942, and despite firm resistance by its Dutch and Australian garrison Amboina fell on 31 January. Thus by the middle of February the Japanese held the northern approaches to Java, and with the collapse of Singapore imminent they struck at Palembang in southeast Sumatra on 16 February, and later took Medan at the opposite end of the island. Further to the east, Dutch-Portuguese Timor fell on 23 February and, using Rabaul in the Bismarck Archipelago as their main advance base, the Japanese occupied Lae and Salamaua on New Guinea on 8 March and Finschhafen on 10 March 1942. Before the end of the month a naval landing force took the three most northerly islands — Buka, Bougainville, and Shortland – in the Solomons chain and began the construction of airfields. These advances brought into sharp focus the very real danger to Australia and the acute need to enlarge its military and naval resources.

ABDACOM's naval responsibilities proved almost as difficult as its missions on land. Admiral Hart assumed command of an Allied naval force, based at Surabaya in western Java, comprising nine cruisers, twenty-six destroyers, and thirty-nine submarines drawn from the US Navy, the Dutch Navy and the Royal Navy. Hart had the almost impossible task of blocking Japanese thrusts against Malaya, the Philippines, Borneo, and into the Molucca Sea, while at the same time defending sea communications between Hawaii, Australia, and New Zealand. Added to these conflicting

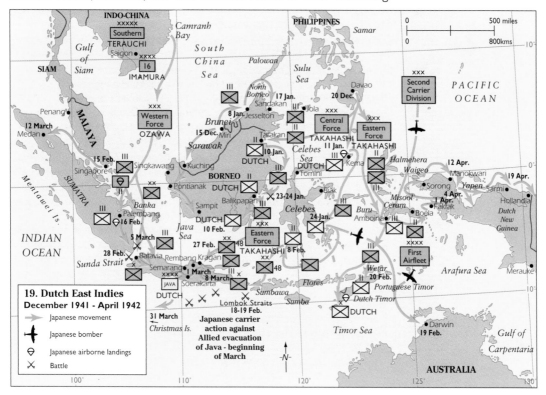

19. Dutch East Indies
December 1941 - April 1942

priorities were the problems of command tension between the senior naval officers in ABDACOM, and strategic disputes thrown up by competing national interests. Yet Hart was keen to fight, and he repeatedly dispatched a cruiser and destroyer strike force to intercept reported Japanese invasion fleets. At Balikpapan his ships finally cornered one and sank seven enemy vessels before retiring without loss. A force of five cruisers and nine destroyers under Dutch Rear Admiral Karel Doorman was less fortunate when it sortied into the Java Sea on 27 February. Doorman, seeking to intercept the troop convoys of the Japanese Eastern Invasion Force on its way to Java, met four cruisers and fourteen destroyers in mid-afternoon. In a running battle which continued into the night, accurate Japanese gunfire and repeated torpedo attacks took a steady toll of the Allied ships. The 8-inch cruiser HMS *Exeter* was hit early in the action and forced to retire to Sourabaya, and the Dutch 6-inch cruisers *De Ruyter* and *Java* were both sunk by torpedoes during the night. The cruisers USS *Houston* and HMAS *Perth* encountered the main Japanese invasion force in the Sunda Strait next day, and although they sank two transports and damaged others, they were themselves sunk after a hopeless but gallant fight. The *Exeter* and two destroyers were intercepted by four Japanese heavy cruisers and three destroyers as they attempted to break out to Colombo, and were sunk after an engagement lasting an hour and a half. Only four of the Allied ships, all American destroyers, that had fought in the Battle of the Java Sea survived. The battle had delayed the invasion of Java by a day.

Java's garrison of some 25,000 Dutch troops plus auxiliaries was supported by a small Allied force comprising a rapidly dwindling number of RAF and RAAF squadrons, two battalions of the 1st Australian Corps lately returned from the Middle East, a squadron of the 3rd Hussars with twenty-five light tanks, Royal Artillery units and one American field artillery regiment. From 3 February 1942, when Japanese air attacks on Java began, they faced overwhelmingly superior enemy power The Japanese deployed two invasion forces against Java, designated as 'Eastern' and 'Western'. The Eastern Force landed during the night of 1 March approximately 100 miles to the west of Sourabaya and quickly advanced southwards. By 8 March the Japanese had occupied Sourabaya and pressed on to the southwest cutting the island in two. The Western Force divided as it approached Java, part of its troops landing at Eretenwetan and part at Bantam Bay and Merak. Once ashore the Japanese made rapid progress towards the capital Bandoeng, and on the morning of 8 March the Dutch Commander-in-Chief, General ter Poorten, surrendered the island. The defence of the Malay barrier had been broken, the Japanese had gained a further supply of precious raw materials, and the Indian Ocean lay open to attack.

Wavell had been given an almost impossible task. The forces assigned to ABDACOM were inadequate for the mission they had been asked to undertake, and almost before it could begin to work effectively as a command structure the Japanese advance had rendered many of its tasks meaningless. Yet in its brief existence ABDACOM, the first unified Allied command of World War II, had demonstrated that the essentials of inter-Allied cooperation could work. It was the model that was to be successfully developed both in the Far East and in other theatres as the war progressed.

On 26 March the Japanese carrier fleet under Admiral Nagumo left Staring Bay in the south of Celebes and sortied into the Indian Ocean. It

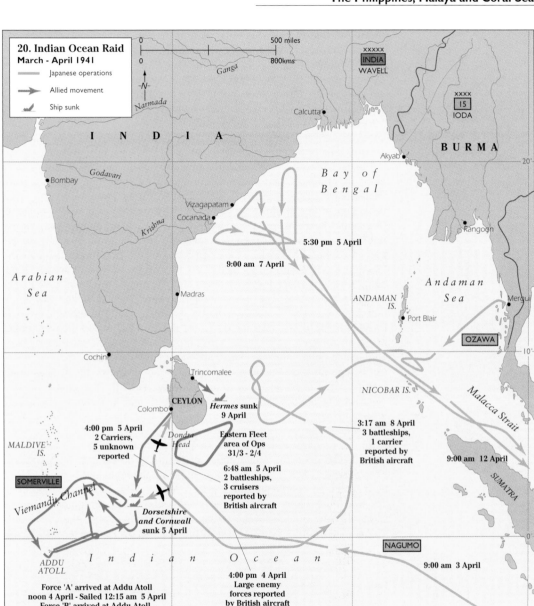

20. Indian Ocean Raid
March - April 1941

Japanese operations

Allied movement

Ship sunk

0 _____ 500 miles

0 _____ 800kms

-N-

Ganga

Narmada

XXXXX
INDIA
WAVELL

XXXX
15
IODA

I N D I A

BURMA

Godavari

•Bombay

Akyab•

20°

Krishna

Vizagapatam•
Cocanada•

B a y   o f
B e n g a l

Rangoon•

5:30 pm 5 April

9:00 am 7 April

A r a b i a n
S e a

•Madras

A n d a m a n
S e a

Merqui•

ANDAMAN
IS.

• Port Blair

OZAWA

Cochin•

NICOBAR IS.

Malacca Strait

Trincomalee•

CEYLON

Hermes sunk
9 April

Colombo•

4:00 pm 5 April
2 Carriers,
5 unknown
reported

*Dondra
Head*

Eastern Fleet
area of Ops
31/3 - 2/4

3:17 am 8 April
3 battleships,
1 carrier
reported by
British aircraft

9:00 am 12 April

MALDIVE
IS.

SUMATRA

6:48 am 5 April
2 battleships,
3 cruisers
reported by
British aircraft

SOMERVILLE

Viemandu Channel

*Dorsetshire
and Cornwall*
sunk 5 April

NAGUMO

9:00 am 3 April

ADDU
ATOLL

I n d i a n   O c e a n

4:00 pm 4 April
Large enemy
forces reported
by British aircraft

Force 'A' arrived at Addu Atoll
noon 4 April - Sailed 12:15 am 5 April
Force 'B' arrived at Addu Atoll
3:00 pm 4 April - Sailed 7:00 am 5 April

80°

90°

100°

10°

0°

consisted of four battleships, five fleet carriers, two heavy cruisers, one
light cruiser, and eight destroyers, while its opponent, the British Eastern
Fleet under Vice Admiral Sir James Somerville, was composed of a fast division of one battleship, two carriers, and six destroyers, and a slow division
of four older battleships, three cruisers, and five destroyers. The Japanese
hoped to destroy the British Fleet and drive the Royal Air Force from the
Bay of Bengal. On 5 April 1942 the Japanese carriers launched an attack
on Colombo in Ceylon and on 9 April on Trincomalee. British aerial reconnaissance had spotted the approach of the Japanese fleet and the two har-
bours had been largely cleared of shipping. The RAF fighters, although

ready for the attack, were overwhelmed and suffered heavy losses. Nagumo, however, failed to find either the British fleet or its anchorage on Addu Atoll, and he had to be content with sinking the heavy cruisers *Dorsetshire* and *Cornwall*, and the carrier *Hermes* all of which were sailing independently. Japanese aircraft, from a second naval force under Vice Admiral Jisaburo Ozawa, operating in the Bay of Bengal sank nearly 100,000 tons of shipping in the first week of April and bombed the Indian coast near Vizagapatam. Japanese submarines added almost a further 40,000 tons of British shipping to this total.

The breakdown of the ABDA Command led to a reorganisation of command in the Pacific and to agreement on a geographical division of responsibility between Great Britain and the United States. From April 1942 Great Britain undertook strategic responsibility for the defence of India, the Indian Ocean and Sumatra, while the United States assumed responsibility for the entire Pacific including China, Australia and New Zealand. The army in the form of General MacArthur took command of the Southwest Pacific Area (SWPA), comprising Australia, the Solomon Islands, the Bismarck Archipelago, New Guinea, the Philippines, Borneo, and the Dutch East Indies except for Sumatra. The navy through Admiral Chester Nimitz took command of the Pacific Ocean Area (POA), which included the remainder of the Pacific except for the approaches to the Panama Canal and the west coast of South America which were designated as the Southeast Pacific Area. The Pacific Ocean Area was subdivided into three further command areas — North, Central, and South — with Nimitz in command of the first two and Vice Admiral Robert Ghormley of the US Navy the third. The command directives issued to MacArthur and Nimitz required them to defend vital military areas, to halt the Japanese advance, and to mount offensives against enemy forces.

Nimitz, spurred on by Admiral King, had already initiated limited offensives based upon the strike power of his three operational fleet carriers, *Enterprise*, *Lexington*, and *Yorktown* (the USS *Saratoga* had been damaged by a Japanese submarine attack on 11 January 1942). Raids by the carriers struck the Gilbert and Marshall Islands, Lae and Salamaua on the north coast of New Guinea, Wake Island, and Marcus Island, the latter only 1,000 miles from Japan. In view of the spirited operational activity of the

A B-25 medium bomber on the flight deck of the USS *Hornet* preparing for take off at the start of the Doolittle Raid.

Pacific Fleet's aircraft carriers the Japanese Navy, in particular, became concerned that they might launch a hit-and-run raid on Tokyo. Although such a raid would not inflict great damage the fact that the emperor's person might be placed in danger would be regarded as a grave dereliction of duty by the navy and army. That this fear became a reality was due largely to Admiral King's operations officer, Captain Francis Low, who had been working on the details of such a raid since January 1942.

To avoid Japanese retaliation the American carriers could not come within 500 miles of Tokyo, and the bombers would have to cover this distance and another 1,500 miles to landing grounds in China. Only planes of the Army Air Force possessed such operational range and twenty-four B-25 Mitchell bombers, under the command of Lieutenant Colonel James Doolittle, were chosen from the 17th Bombardment Group. The B-25s, which would carry a 2,000-pound bomb load, were fitted with auxiliary fuel tanks to provide a capacity of 1,141 gallons. After a brief period of training in taking-off in a distance equivalent to the flight deck of a carrier, the bombers and their crews arrived at Alameda Naval Air Station in San Francisco Bay on 31 March amidst great secrecy.

Captain Marc Mitscher, the commander of the USS *Hornet*, talks with Major General Doolittle and some of the airmen who took part in the historic first air raid against Japan in April 1942.

Sixteen B-25s, all that could be accommodated, were loaded aboard the newly commissioned USS *Hornet* and on 2 April the carrier, escorted by two cruisers, four destroyers and a tanker, set sail for a rendezvous with a second carrier, the USS *Enterprise*, which would provide fighter cover for the voyage. After the carriers joined forces north of Midway on 13 April, the task force, under the command of Vice Admiral William F. Halsey Jr., headed through the heavy seas of the north Pacific towards a launch position some 450 miles from Tokyo. On 18 April the carriers were reported by an enemy picket boat stationed 700 miles east of Japan, and in order to minimise the risk to his carriers Halsey decided to launch the bombers without delay; a day early and 200 miles further from their target than planned. By 9.24 am Colonel Doolittle's B-25s were airborne and the carriers set a course for Pearl Harbor at twenty-five knots.

The flight of the B-25s to Tokyo was undisturbed by the enemy and at 12.15 pm (Tokyo time) Doolittle's plane, with two others, dropped its bomb load on the city. At 12.40 pm a second group of eleven bombers arrived over Tokyo and struck oil storage depots, factories, generating plants, mili-

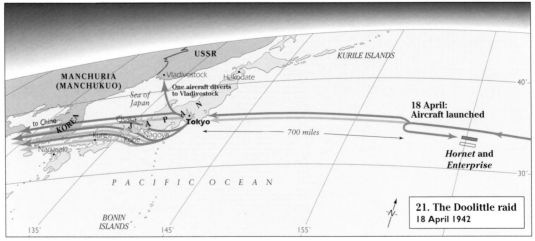

21. The Doolittle raid
18 April 1942

tary buildings and, accidentally, some civilian targets. The final three aircraft dropped incendiaries on Kobe, Nagoya, Yokohama and the Yokosuka Navy Yard. Not a single bomber was shot down and most of the crews made landfall in China. Seventy-one of the eighty men involved in the raid survived the mission. Japanese attempts to intercept the *Hornet* and the *Enterprise* with land-based bombers and their own fleet carriers were unsuccessful, and the American task force returned safely to Pearl Harbor on 25 April. The physical damage to Tokyo was slight but the raid had a significant effect upon morale both in Japan and the United States. Amidst a sequence of disaster and defeat, and only nine days after the surrender on Bataan, the American public had at last something to celebrate. The raid represented a humiliating loss of face for the military leadership in Japan, and it was a clear indication to the Japanese people that the much vaunted defensive cordon of the empire could be breached by the United States, almost at will. Thereafter fear for the safety of the home islands was to exert a considerable influence on Japanese strategic planning.

Tactical raids by carriers, while inflicting casualties on the enemy's garrisons and damaging the strength and capability of his shipping and air power, had not stopped the Japanese advance. Only a strategic defeat could achieve this and an opportunity for such an operation presented itself in the South Pacific in April 1942. American Intelligence intercepts of the Japanese naval code JN25 revealed that the enemy was planning to advance on Tulagi in the Solomons, and Port Moresby on the south coast of Papua New Guinea, both of which were held by Australian forces. By the beginning of May a task force based around the carriers *Yorktown*, and *Lexington*, and including an Australian cruiser squadron under Rear Admiral

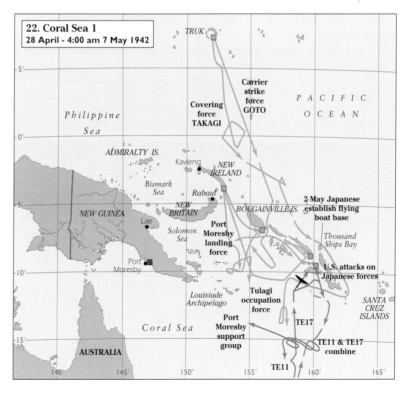

22. Coral Sea 1
28 April - 4:00 am 7 May 1942

Sir John Grace RN, had assembled in the Coral Sea to oppose the Japanese units heading for Port Moresby. The carriers *Hornet* and *Enterprise*, only lately returned from the Doolittle raid, were ordered south from Pearl Harbor to join the task force, but as they had to steam some 3,500 miles it was doubtful whether they would arrive in time.

While the task force was refuelling at sea, Rear Admiral Frank J Fletcher, commanding from the *Yorktown*, learnt that the Japanese had landed at Tulagi after the weak Australian garrison had been withdrawn. Taking the *Yorktown* and supporting units Fletcher sped north to attack the Japanese invasion fleet. A strike from the *Yorktown* against Tulagi on 4 May found that the enemy covering force had already withdrawn and only a destroyer, a transport, and two patrol boats were sunk. Rejoining the *Lexington* and Admiral Grace's squadron, Fletcher sailed northwest towards the Jomard Passage between the eastern tip of New Guinea and the Louisiade Archipelago on 6 May. He hoped to intercept the invasion convoy as it came through the Passage and he dispatched Admiral Grace's squadron to close the southern exit. Meanwhile Fletcher's aircraft searched the Coral Sea for signs of the Japanese carriers.

The invasion convoy was escorted by the light carrier *Shoho*, four heavy cruisers, and a number of destroyers, but a separate task force of two fleet carriers, the *Zuikaku* and *Shokaku*, and two heavy cruisers, commanded by Rear Admiral Takagi, had entered the Coral Sea during 5 May and was now behind the American task force and only some seventy miles to the northeast. On the morning of 7 May the reconnaissance planes of both task forces reported that they had found the enemy fleet carriers, but both reports were incorrect. The Americans had located the *Shoho*, and the

Admiral Osami Nagano, Chief of the Japanese Navy General Staff.

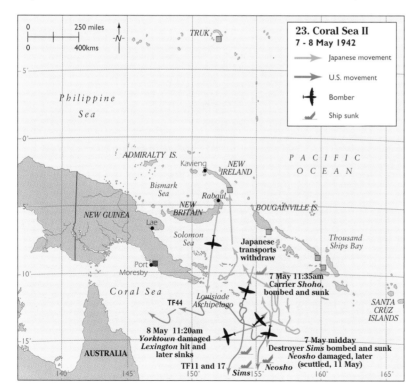

Japanese had in fact sighted only a tanker and its destroyer escort which had been sent south by Fletcher to seek safety away from the main action. All three ships, Japanese and American, were sunk by carrier aircraft. The Australian squadron also came in for attention by Japanese bombers but through skilful manoeuvring managed to survive without loss.

At about 8.00 am on 8 May both task forces at last found their opposite numbers, after almost three days of reconnaissance. Air strikes were launched from the *Yorktown* and *Lexington* but Admiral Takagi had made excellent use of a storm front to hide his carriers and only the *Shokaku* was visible when the American planes reached their reported position. SDB Dauntless dive bombers registered three hits on the *Shokaku*, reducing her flight deck to a shambles. Unable to operate aircraft, the carrier withdrew from the action. Meanwhile, Takagi's own strike aircraft had found Fletcher's carriers under clear skies and with their defences weakened by the absence of Grace's cruisers. Moreover, only fifteen American fighters were available as a combat air patrol. Seventy Japanese aircraft roared down on the carriers scoring a bomb and two torpedo hits on the *Lexington* and a bomb hit on the *Yorktown*. For the moment both carriers remained in action, but at 12.47 pm an explosion caused by fuel vapour started additional fires on the *Lexington*, and two hours later a second explosion spread the fires till they raged out of control. Late in the afternoon of 8 May the crew abandoned ship and a destroyer sent the *Lexington* to the bottom with torpedoes.

Fletcher, his strike force reduced to one fleet carrier and about forty aircraft, decided that his only course was to withdraw, a decision later confirmed by Nimitz. Takagi's offensive power had also been more than halved and his superior at Rabaul, Admiral Shigeyoshi Inoue, believed that the *Zuikaku* alone was not sufficient to cover the invasion. In addition to the ships that had been sunk or damaged, the Japanese lost seventy-seven aircraft and 1,074 personnel, while American casualties were 543 killed or wounded and sixty-six planes destroyed. Both task forces withdrew from the Coral Sea and the Japanese assault on Port Moresby was postponed. The first battle in naval history to be conducted entirely by carrier aircraft and in which neither of the contending fleets came within sight of the other was over. In terms of tonnage sunk the Japanese had secured a tactical victory, but at the strategic level they had suffered a serious defeat. Port Moresby had been saved and for the first time in World War II the Japanese had failed to achieve their objective.

Douglas TBD-1 Devastator torpedo bombers on the USS *Enterprise* just before they took off for Midway. The Devastator was already obsolete at the start of the fighting in the Pacific and it fell an easy prey to the Japanese Zero.

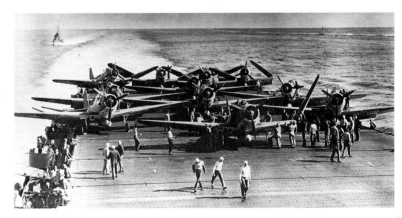

4 Seizing the Initiative: Midway

Although Japan had reaped in full the advantages of a first strike, her pre-war strategic planning for what would happen next was unsophisticated and essentially negative. Once the initial period of conquest was complete, and American strength in the Far East reduced, the navy for one had been able to present no more cogent strategy than to simply preserve the new *status quo* by defeating American fleets as they pressed westwards. Eventually Japan hoped the United States, distracted by the war in Europe, would tire of its losses and seek a negotiated peace. This strategic vacuum was due largely to the fact that Japanese planning had been driven by the acquisition of sources of oil, and also because the risks involved in the opening operations were considered so high that detailed long term planning was seen as premature. In short the Japanese had been taken by surprise by their own success. Their achievement had indeed been impressive. In a little over five months Japan had conquered Hong Kong, Siam, Malaya, Burma, the Philippines, the Dutch East Indies, Guam, Wake, and the Bismarck Archipelago. The Combined Fleet, in the process of sweeping the Pacific and Indian Oceans from Pearl Harbor to Ceylon, had sunk five enemy battleships (and damaged several more), 2 aircraft carriers, 7 cruisers, and numerous smaller warships. In addition to the thousands of their troops who had been killed or wounded, the Allies had lost 250,000 men as prisoners of war. For the gains made Japan's losses had been remarkably light.

The choice facing the Japanese planners in the spring of 1942 appeared deceptively straightforward: should they stand on the defensive and attempt to hold their strategic gains, or should they resume the offensive in a bid to break the Allies will to fight? If the latter, should they attack British interests first or those of the United States? The strategic debate which took place around these issues was largely promoted by the navy since the army, feeling its resources already overstretched in the southern area, had begun to speculate on what might be achieved by an attack on Russia should the Germans break through in Europe on the Eastern Front. The development of strategic policy was the responsibility of the navy and army General Staffs functioning as part of Imperial General Headquarters. In theory, naval operational policy originated from the office of the Chief of the Navy General Staff, was confirmed by Imperial General Headquarters, and was then executed by the Commander-in-Chief, Combined Fleet. In practice, however, the Combined Fleet often usurped the role of strategic planner. The attack on Pearl Harbor had gone ahead against the wishes of the Navy General Staff because Admiral Yamamoto, Commander-in-Chief Combined Fleet, had insisted that it should. In developing the navy's strategy for the second phase of operations the prime mover was once again the Combined Fleet.

The possibility of defeating the United States outright was never considered by Japan for it was correctly felt to be beyond the nation's resources, even with the addition of the Greater East Asian Co-Prosperity Sphere. Instead, and in the absence of established plans for exploiting the favourable situation in the Pacific, the High Command succumbed to what Japanese staff officers were later to describe as 'victory disease'. Rather than consolidate their early conquests and prepare for a long-term defensive phase of operations, the Japanese decided to attack. Thus although committed to a limited war in the Pacific, the Japanese now took steps to ensure that it became unlimited.

The detailed strategic options that were considered by Rear Admiral Matome Ugaki, the Chief of Staff of the Combined Fleet, involved the choice of operations to the west against India and Ceylon, to the south against Australia, or to the east against Hawaii. The objectives of an attack westwards would be the destruction of the British Eastern Fleet, the occupation of Ceylon, and the elimination of British air power over the Indian Ocean. It also held the prospect, however remote, of cooperation with German forces advancing eastwards. If these aims could be achieved the security of the Japanese position in Malaya and the Dutch East Indies would be reinforced. This scheme foundered because it was not acceptable to the army, which looked with concern at the manpower requirements for the invasion of Ceylon. Turning next to the southeast the Combined Fleet considered the strategic advantages of a descent upon Australia.

With the loss of the Philippines it was vital to the Allies that Australia and the bases on the line of communication stretching northeastwards via Hawaii towards the United States should be held. During the battle for the Philippines a resupply convoy of seven ships, escorted by the cruiser, USS *Pensacola*, had arrived in Brisbane on 22 December 1941 as the focus of a new command entitled US Army Forces in Australia (USAFIA). Under the command of Major General George Brett, who reported to General MacArthur, USAFIA would become an air and supply base charged with running supplies to the Philippines. In fact the speed of the Japanese advance meant that very few supplies ever reached MacArthur, but the importance of Australia as a base for the build-up of American strength in the south Pacific had been clearly demonstrated. In January 1942 the United States began to rush garrisons to the islands that would form staging and defence posts along the line of communications between Australia, New Zealand, and Hawaii on route to the West Coast and Panama. A marine brigade landed on American Samoa and 15,000 infantry, supported by tanks, artillery and a fighter squadron, were sent to reinforce the Free French and Australians on New Caledonia. Technicians, engineers, fighting men, fuel and supplies were dispatched by convoy via the Panama Canal to Palmyra, Christmas, and Canton Islands, and construction work began on a naval support base at Bora Bora in the Society Islands. New Zealand troops and a United States fighter squadron reinforced the garrison of Fiji, and an Australian brigade dug in to defend Port Moresby. Bases were also constructed on Espiritu Santo in the north of the New Hebrides and at Efate in the south, and a garrison was provided for Tongatabu in the Friendly Islands. On 14 February 1942 the United States committed itself to the defence of Australia with the decision that infantry and supporting troops would be stationed in the subcontinent. In March the forward echelon of the 41st United States Division left San Francisco for Sydney. The Australian 5th and 6th Infantry Divisions were recalled from the fighting in the Middle East to further bolster the Allies' defences.

The reinforcement of the south Pacific line of communications and the defence of Australia were necessary measures which could not be delayed, but they went against established Allied policy. At the ARCADIA Conference convened in Washington late in December 1941, Great Britain and the

United States had confirmed that the defeat of Germany was their first priority. They had also agreed that the resources allocated to the Far East would be limited to those necessary to hold areas required for the staging of an eventual offensive against Japan, and to support China's active participation in the war. Many planners, especially in the United States Army, felt that the emphasis placed on the Pacific violated this strategy, and while it could be argued that the measures taken were purely defensive, an ever higher proportion of the shipping and aircraft available to the Allies was being deployed against Japan rather than Germany. Writing towards the end of January 1942, General Dwight D Eisenhower, the Chief of the War Plans Division, was already concerned that the Allies were spreading their resources too thinly and in the wrong direction:

'We've got to go to Europe and fight; we've got to quit wasting resources all over the world — and still worse — wasting time.'

The US Navy, and Admiral King in particular, disagreed. While they acknowledged the need for an offensive in Europe, navy planners believed that the fleet's line of communications with Australia and the South Pacific must be secured as a priority. Without this vital preliminary it would be almost impossible to halt the Japanese advance. Once this had been achieved, however, King felt that the United States could assume the offensive by following Japan's strategy of a step-by-step, island-by-island, advance. From the New Hebrides the Allies could push northwestwards to take the Solomons and then the Bismarck Archipelago. The army, with the exception of General MacArthur who wanted as high a percentage of resources for his theatre of war as possible, countered by arguing that risks must be taken in the Pacific in order to further the Allied offensive in Europe. In April 1942 the United States insisted that the Allies should prepare for an invasion of continental Europe in 1943 (ROUNDUP), and even earlier if Russia appeared to be on the brink of collapse (SLEDGE-HAMMER). To meet this timetable United States forces had to start their deployment in Great Britain without delay (BOLERO). In May 1942 the president settled the argument between the services. BOLERO would go ahead. Once the forces in the Pacific had been brought up to their authorised strength, priority for resources would rest with the European theatre.

Australia's importance to the Allies was obvious to the Japanese and they rightly feared that unless action was taken, the subcontinent would become the springboard for the American assault on their southern defensive perimeter. Their concern was so great that on 19 February 1942 over 200 Japanese bombers and fighters attacked the port and town of Darwin on Australia's northwest coast. The aircraft had come from Admiral Nagumo's four fleet carriers and from the 21st Air Flotilla at Kendari on Celebes. The carriers sortied from Palau, crossed the Banda Sea at night and launched their aircraft in the Timor Sea. The Allies lost eleven ships in Darwin harbour, twenty-three aircraft on the airbase, and suffered over 500 casualties. The raids on Darwin and other northwest ports did not, however, provide a long term solution, and a number of officers on the Navy General Staff argued that Japan must invade Australia and occupy key areas of the subcontinent. The Army moved quickly to squash this proposal stating bluntly that the ten divisions required for this enterprise were simply not available.

The Combined Fleet was still convinced that Japan must strike somewhere if the Allies were to be kept off balance, and it proposed that an offensive to the east against Midway Atoll, with a diversionary attack on the western Aleutians, should be mounted early in June 1942. The Navy General Staff responded by suggesting an advance on New Caledonia, Fiji and Samoa. This would cut US communications with Australia and prevent the subcontinent being used as the base for a counteroffensive. The Combined Fleet argued that if Midway was threatened the US Pacific Fleet, and most importantly its carriers, would sail to the island's defence. The Japanese would then finish the work they had begun at Pearl Harbor, gain their own advance bases on Midway and the Aleutians, and lay the enemy's communications bare. Yamamoto, who was deeply worried by the prospect of United States carrier attacks on the Japanese home islands, threw his authority and prestige behind the Midway operation. The Navy General Staff reluctantly agreed that it should have first priority, but protested that June was an impossible deadline for the attack. While the argument was finely balanced Lieutenant Colonel James Doolittle led his B-25s to Tokyo and settled the matter once and for all. The American fleet carriers were a thorn in the side of the Japanese Navy and their demise was long overdue. As the Combined Fleet could no longer risk sailing into Pearl Harbor an attack on Midway would be the next best thing. The army raised no lasting objections since the invasion of Midway would require only one reinforced infantry regiment. On 5 May 1942 Admiral Osami Nagano, Chief of the Navy General Staff, issued orders to Admiral Yamamoto to carry out the operations against Midway (MI) and the Aleutians (AL).

Throughout the planning and execution of the Midway operation, Japanese actions were permeated by an arrogance born of their unrestricted success during the first months of the Pacific War. They steadfastly believed that they would retain the initiative during the attack, and that the United States Navy would limit itself to mere reaction to Japanese moves. The Combined Fleet was also convinced that the United States would remain in ignorance of Japanese plans until after the first strike on Midway. In reality, by early April 1942, United States Naval Intelligence teams in Melbourne, Hawaii, and Washington were aware of a forthcoming large-scale enemy operation through their success in deciphering the Japanese Navy's code JN25. Although the United States could not understand the complete code, the American combat intelligence group led by Commander Joseph Rochefort in Hawaii was able to decipher sufficient Japanese signal traffic to conclude that Midway was the next target. Other intelligence teams were not convinced that Hawaii's estimation was correct, but Nimitz backed Rochefort's view and he was able to persuade Admiral King that the navy's fleet carriers should be concentrated to defend Midway. As Vice Admiral William Halsey was hospitalised through illness, the command of the carrier task force devolved upon Rear Admiral Fletcher with Rear Admiral Raymond Spruance as his second-in-command. With the *Enterprise* and *Hornet*, five cruisers and nine destroyers designated as Task Force 16, Spruance sortied from Hawaii on 28 May. Fletcher was delayed at Pearl Harbor due to the battle damage inflicted on the *Yorktown* at the Coral Sea. Although the necessary repairs had been estimated at three months dockyard time, the *Yorktown* was operational within two days and she put to sea on 29 May as Task Force 17 with a screen of two cruisers and six destroyers. Thanks to further JN25 decrypts Nimitz had been able to provide Fletcher with the Japanese order of battle for the Midway attack, and the direction from which the they would approach the Atoll.

The Japanese plan for the forthcoming operations, particularly in relation to Midway was overly complex. More than 200 ships, comprising eleven battleships, including the 60,000 ton super-battleship *Yamato*, eight carriers, twenty-two cruisers, sixty-five destroyers, and twenty-one submarines, were deployed in five separate commands: Main Force (Admiral Yamamoto), First Carrier Striking Force, Midway Invasion Force, Northern Aleutians Force, and the Advance Submarine Force. Between 26–29 May the ships in these commands sailed from three widely dispersed assembly points: Saipan and Guam in the Mariana Islands, Ominato on north Honshu, and Hashirajima in Hiroshima Bay. They were supported by a sixth command, Shore-Based Air Force, under Vice Admiral Nishizo Tsukahara, which would operate a group of 214 fighters and bombers from island bases in the central Pacific.

Although 7 June 1942, when the main landing on Midway would take place, was the key date in the overall plan, the diversion in the Aleutians was set to commence on 3 June (Aleutian time) in the hope that it would draw the Americans northwards. The operation involved landings on the Islands of Adak, Attu, and Kiska, an attack on United States installations at Dutch Harbor on the Island of Unalaska, and then a withdrawal by mid-September before winter conditions set in. The Northern Aleutians Force,

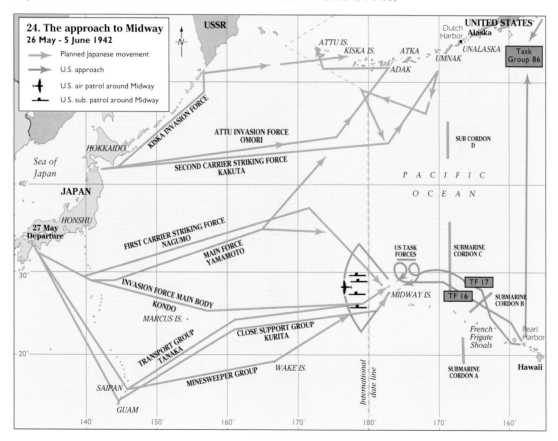

under Vice Admiral Moshiro Hosogaya, was built around the carriers *Ryujo* and *Junyo* (the Second Carrier Striking Force – Rear Admiral Kakuji Kakuta) with seventy-two aircraft. At 2.43 am on 3 June, fifteen minutes before sunrise and with the temperature at –7° Centigrade, twenty-three bombers and twelve fighters were launched from the carriers for a strike against Dutch Harbor. Only a proportion of the aircraft reached the target and little damage was caused. More importantly, the United States, already aware of the impending assault on Midway, did not allow their attention to be diverted from the central Pacific in the slightest.

The Combined Fleet's Midway operation, which was predicated on the belief that any intervention by the United States Fleet would take place only after the assault landings, was planned as two main phases: the bombardment and assault, and then the fleet encounter. On 5 June aircraft from Admiral Nagumo's First Carrier Striking Force would attack Midway to destroy American air strength, land defences, and shipping. Then on 7 June the Transport Group of the Midway Invasion Force (Vice Admiral Nobutake Kondo) would land troops on Sand and Eastern Islands, which together make up Midway Atoll. While the landings were in progress the battleships and cruisers of the Combined Fleet would close up ready for the decisive fleet battle. One of the major problems for the Japanese was the difficulty in gaining intelligence on the strength and direction of the American response. They assumed it would be mounted from Hawaii and took the precaution of deploying the Advance Submarine Force, under Vice Admiral Teruhisa Komatsu, in three advanced cordons, designed to detect approaching enemy fleet units. To supplement this screen a reconnaissance mission flown by two 'Kawanishi' Type-2 flying boats would proceed to Hawaii, having refuelled on route from submarines waiting at French Frigate Shoals, 500 miles northwest of Oahu. In the event, this mission failed and two of the submarine cordons were late in forming. As a result

The *Mikuma*, a Japanese Mogami class heavy cruiser, reduced to a burning wreck by United States aircraft during the Battle of Midway. Captain R E Fleming USMC inflicted significant damage on the *Mikuma* when he deliberately crashed his crippled dive bomber into the cruiser.

Nagumo's four carriers, *Akagi, Hiryu, Kaga,* and *Soryu,* steaming steadily eastwards, were in the dark as to the location and intentions of Task Forces 16 and 17, and woefully unaware of the reception the United States forces were preparing for them.

On 2 June the *Yorktown* rendezvoused with the *Enterprise* and *Hornet* some 350 miles to the northeast of Midway, and proceeded to close to a position 200 miles to the north of the Atoll. Fletcher's basic tactic was to avoid an encounter with major Japanese surface units and to concentrate on air action against the enemy carriers. On 3 June the Japanese invasion force had been spotted some 700 miles west of Midway by a reconnaissance Catalina flown by Ensign Jack Reid. Army Air Force B-17s were scrambled to intercept the Japanese transports, but neither this nor subsequent attacks from Midway inflicted more than psychological damage on the enemy. Fletcher, however, was approaching the perfect ambush position, ready to take Nagumo's carriers in flank while they were occupied in attacking Midway.

Before dawn on 4 June, Nagumo launched approximately half his strike aircraft against Midway from a position roughly 240 miles to the northwest of the Atoll. At the same time seven search planes were due to take off to reconnoitre 300 miles out from the carriers. It was to be a single phase reconnaissance with only one plane covering each search pattern, and the aircraft from the battleship *Haruna* had a range of only 150 miles. Thus if any plane missed a sighting there would be no second aircraft covering the same route, an hour or so later, which could rectify the omission. By 4.30 am the search planes, with the exception of those from the heavy cruisers *Tone* and *Chikuma* were airborne, hunting for any sign of an American surface force. Another thirty minutes were to pass before the last two search planes took off, a delay that had fatal consequences for Nagumo's force.

As the Japanese bombers and fighters were on route to attack Midway, Nagumo's carriers were spotted by American reconnaissance planes. American fighters were immediately launched from Midway. Although the twenty-five Buffalo and Wildcat fighters of Marine Squadron VMF-221 on Midway were outclassed by the Zero, they succeeded, together with the Atoll's anti-aircraft guns, in knocking down six of the attacking planes and damaging a number more. Midway's bombers soon found the Japanese carriers and although they did not score any hits they kept Nagumo's fleet off-balance and uncertain as to what to expect next.

While these attacks were underway Nagumo learnt from his own strike planes that a second bombing raid on Midway would be required. Orders were given for the aircraft held back on the carriers to be rearmed with fragmentation bombs in place of the armour-piercing ordnance and torpedoes they carried to attack warships. While the Japanese planes were below deck and in the process of rearming, a message sent at 7.28 am from the *Tone's* delayed search plane was received announcing the sighting of an American surface fleet some 240 miles north of Midway. This sighting caused consternation among Nagumo's staff since the presence of an enemy surface force barely 200 miles away had not been anticipated at such an early stage in the assault on Midway. At 7.45 am Admiral Nagumo ordered that the bombers, which were in the middle of rearming, should switch back to anti-shipping ordnance. At about 8.30 am, while Nagumo was weighing the risk of attacking the enemy surface fleet while the majority of his fighters were occupied elsewhere, the Midway attack force returned to the carriers. Nagumo decided to recover these planes and re-group his ships before launching a strike on the American task force. With this decision he sealed the fate of his own carriers.

Away to the northeast Fletcher and Spruance were determined to attack the Japanese carriers at the earliest opportunity even though, at approximately 150 miles, the range to the target was greater than they would have wished. So anxious was Spruance to catch Nagumo unawares, that at 8.00 am he ordered the thirty-three SBD Dauntless dive bombers from the *Enterprise* which were already airborne, to head for the Japanese carriers without fighter escort. The *Hornet's* dive bombers and fighters set off next and they were followed by the remaining SBDs and Wildcats from the *Enterprise*. The attack force was thus split into four separate groups each of which was heading for Nagumo's last reported position. It was assumed that the Japanese carriers were still steaming southeast towards Midway, whereas in fact they had turned to the north to close with Task Forces 16 and 17. The dive bombers and fighters from the *Hornet* missed Nagumo completely and were forced to turn back to the carrier or land on Midway. Many of the fighters ran out of fuel before they touched down and had to ditch at sea. Lieutenant Commander John Waldron, leading the Devastator torpedo bombers of VT-8 from the *Hornet*, turned to the northwest rather than to the south and found Nagumo at 9.20 am. Waldron's squadron was

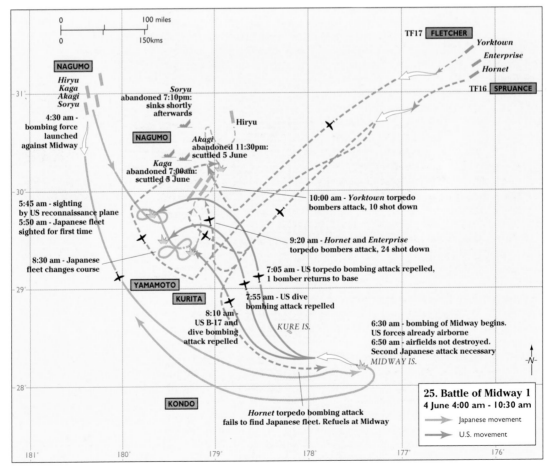

25. Battle of Midway 1
4 June 4:00 am - 10:30 am

→ Japanese movement
➡ U.S. movement

TF17 **FLETCHER**
Yorktown
Enterprise
Hornet
TF16 **SPRUANCE**

NAGUMO
Hiryu
Kaga
Akagi
Soryu

4:30 am -
bombing force
launched
against Midway

Soryu
abandoned 7:10pm:
sinks shortly
afterwards

Hiryu

NAGUMO
Akagi
abandoned 11:30pm:
scuttled 5 June

Kaga
abandoned 7:00am:
scuttled 5 June

5:45 am - sighting
by US reconnaissance plane
5:50 am - Japanese fleet
sighted for first time

10:00 am - *Yorktown* torpedo
bombers attack, 10 shot down

8:30 am - Japanese
fleet changes course

9:20 am - *Hornet* and *Enterprise*
torpedo bombers attack, 24 shot down

YAMAMOTO

7:05 am - US torpedo bombing attack repelled,
1 bomber returns to base

KURITA

7:55 am - US dive
bombing attack repelled

8:10 am -
US B-17 and
dive bombing
attack repelled

KURE IS.

6:30 am - bombing of Midway begins.
US forces already airborne
6:50 am - airfields not destroyed.
Second Japanese attack necessary
MIDWAY IS.

KONDO

Hornet torpedo bombing attack
fails to find Japanese fleet. Refuels at Midway

pounced upon by the fifty Zeros mounting the combat air patrol over the Japanese fleet and within minutes all fifteen of his planes had been shot down. The fourteen Devastators of VT-6 were the next American planes to arrive and all but four were eliminated by the Japanese fighters. A further twelve torpedo bombers, from the *Yorktown*'s VT-3, then deployed to attack the enemy carriers but this time in a tactical grouping with support from dive bombers and fighters. Only two of the torpedo bombers survived and as yet not a single enemy ship had been hit.

Nagumo's four carriers were at last ready to launch their own strike and their decks were crowded with fully armed and fuelled planes waiting for the signal to take off. At this moment thirty-three SDB dive bombers from the *Enterprise*, led by Lieutenant Commander Wade McClusky, appeared out of the clouds and hurtled down on the Japanese carriers. The defending Zeros, which had just dealt with the American torpedo bombers, were still at low altitude and could not climb fast enough to halt this latest attack. McClusky's bombers were joined by those of Lieutenant Commander Maxwell Leslie from the *Yorktown* and within minutes the carriers *Kaga*, *Akagi*, and *Soryu* had been reduced to cauldrons of exploding bombs, aircraft, and fuel. The Japanese aircrews were blown to pieces or incinerated where they sat in their planes.

As the American aircraft turned away, the surviving Japanese carrier, the

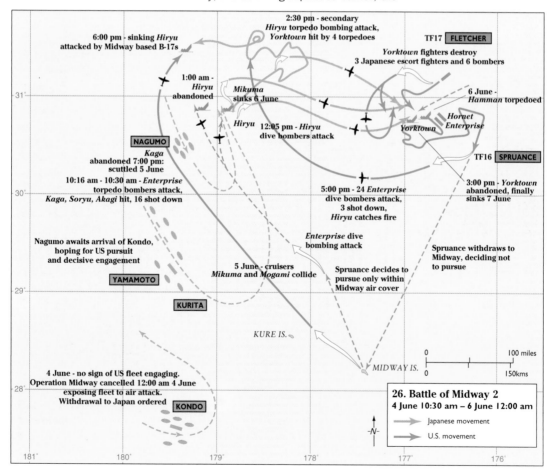

2:30 pm - secondary
Hiryu torpedo bombing attack,
Yorktown hit by 4 torpedoes

6:00 pm - sinking *Hiryu*
attacked by Midway based B-17s

TF17 FLETCHER

Yorktown fighters destroy
3 Japanese escort fighters and 6 bombers

1:00 am -
Hiryu
abandoned

Mikuma
sinks 6 June

6 June -
Hamman torpedoed

31°

Hiryu 12:05 pm - *Hiryu*
dive bombers attack

Hornet
Enterprise

Yorktown

NAGUMO

Kaga
abandoned 7:00 pm:
scuttled 5 June

TF16 SPRUANCE

10:16 am - 10:30 am - *Enterprise*
torpedo bombers attack,
Kaga, Soryu, Akagi hit, 16 shot down

5:00 pm - 24 *Enterprise*
dive bombers attack,
3 shot down,
Hiryu catches fire

3:00 pm - *Yorktown*
abandoned, finally
sinks 7 June

30°

Enterprise dive
bombing attack

Nagumo awaits arrival of Kondo,
hoping for US pursuit
and decisive engagement

Spruance withdraws to
Midway, deciding not
to pursue

YAMAMOTO

5 June - cruisers
Mikuma and *Mogami* collide

Spruance decides to
pursue only within
Midway air cover

29°

KURITA

KURE IS.

0   100 miles

4 June - no sign of US fleet engaging.
Operation Midway cancelled 12:00 am 4 June
exposing fleet to air attack.
Withdrawal to Japan ordered

MIDWAY IS.

0   150kms

28°

KONDO

26. Battle of Midway 2
4 June 10:30 am – 6 June 12:00 am

-N-

Japanese movement

U.S. movement

181°   180°   179°   178°   177°   176°

Hiryu, launched a strike by forty-six torpedo and dive bombers escorted by twelve fighters. After following a number of American planes as they returned to the *Yorktown*, the Japanese were intercepted by fighters, but the carrier was hit by three bombs. For a time the *Yorktown* was dead in the water, and as she regained power two torpedoes from *Hiryu's* aircraft struck on the port side and a list developed. The carrier was critically damaged and her crew abandoned ship. She remained afloat for another two days, and was taken under tow by the minesweeper USS *Vireo*, only to be sunk by four torpedoes from the Japanese submarine *I-168*. The *Hiryu*, in turn, was found in the afternoon of 4 June by bombers from the American carriers and damaged to the extent that she had to be sunk the next day by Japanese destroyers. With Nagumo's carriers gone, Yamamoto believed that his best chance of exacting vengeance on Fletcher and Spruance was by a night surface action, when the American carriers would be largely ineffective. While battle raged between the carrier task forces on 4 June, the battleships and cruisers of Yamamoto's Main Force were still 800 miles to the northwest of Midway. Before he could attack, Yamamoto had to concentrate the ships of the various dispersed Japanese commands and close with the American carriers. Accordingly he suspended the proposed landings on Midway, ordered Admiral Kakuta with the carriers *Ryujo* and *Junyo*, then 120 miles southwest of Dutch Harbor in the Aleutians, to steam south, and set the warships of Admiral Kondo's Invasion Force and the First Carrier Striking Force in pursuit of Task Forces 16 and 17. Realising that such an attack was a possibility, Spruance had temporarily withdrawn his ships to the east before swinging west again after midnight. It quickly became apparent that Kakuta's carriers would not reach the Midway area before 8 June, and that with the American withdrawal the possibility of forcing an early night action was remote. At 2.55 am on 5 June 1942 Yamamoto, acknowledging the inevitable, abandoned the Midway operation and ordered a general retirement to the west. Only the tragedy of Cruiser Division 7's bombardment mission against Midway remained to be played out. The four heavy cruisers – *Kumano*, *Mikuma*, *Mogami*, and *Suzuya* – of Rear Admiral Takeo Kurita's Support Force had been detached to carry out a night gun attack on Midway's airfields and installations. While the cruisers were steaming towards the Atoll they sighted the American submarine *Tambor*, and during the evasive action which followed the *Mikuma* and *Mogami* collided at 28 knots. Shortly afterwards the mission was cancelled and the damaged cruisers, retiring westwards, were found next day by bombers from the *Enterprise* and *Hornet* who sank the *Mikuma* and badly damaged the *Mogami*. Declining to be drawn into range of the Japanese bombers stationed on Wake, Spruance turned eastwards and set a course for Pearl Harbor on the evening of 6 June.

The USS *Yorktown* (CV 5) is abandoned by its crew at Midway, after hits by enemy bombs and torpedoes.

The Japanese carrier *Hiryu* at Midway, on fire after an attack by American dive bombers. This bow view of the *Hiryu* was taken by an aircraft from the light carrier *Hosho* which had been sent to search for Admiral Nagumo's ships by Yamamoto.

The Japanese operation against Midway had resulted in a disastrous failure. The Combined Fleet had lost four of its best carriers and hundreds of its most skilful and experienced aircrews; on the *Hiryu* alone 130 out of 150 pilots became casualties. These were losses which neither Japanese industry nor its air training programme could replace, and they represented a turning point in the war in the Pacific. Though there would still be crises to be surmounted in the future, a decisive battle had been won by the US Navy at Midway. The Japanese Combined Fleet, despite its considerable remaining strength, was now irretrievably on the defensive. The strategic pulse in the Pacific was to rest increasingly with the United States.

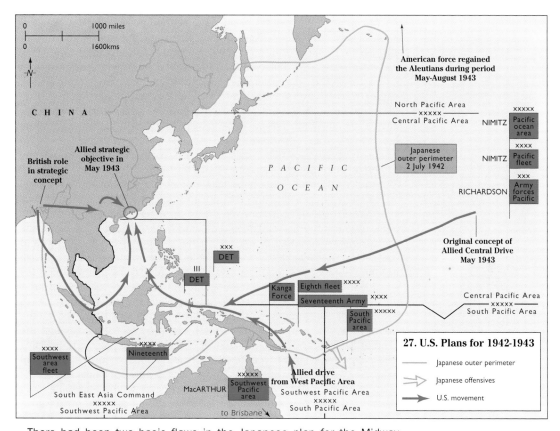

0   1000 miles

0   1600kms

-N-

C H I N A

American force regained the Aleutians during period May-August 1943

North Pacific Area
xxxxx
Central Pacific Area   NIMITZ

xxxxx   Pacific ocean area

xxxx   Pacific fleet

British role in strategic concept

Allied strategic objective in May 1943

Japanese outer perimeter 2 July 1942   NIMITZ

P A C I F I C

O C E A N

RICHARDSON   xxx   Army forces Pacific

Original concept of Allied Central Drive May 1943

xxx   DET

III   DET

Kanga Force   Eighth fleet   xxxx

Seventeenth Army   xxxx

South Pacific area   xxxxx

Central Pacific Area
xxxxx
South Pacific Area

27. U.S. Plans for 1942-1943

Japanese outer perimeter

Japanese offensives

U.S. movement

xxxx   Southwest area fleet

xxxx   Nineteenth

South East Asia Command
xxxxx
Southwest Pacific Area

MacARTHUR   xxxxx   Southwest Pacific area

Allied drive from West Pacific Area   Southwest Pacific Area
xxxxx
South Pacific Area

to Brisbane

There had been two basic flaws in the Japanese plan for the Midway operation: an outdated belief that battleships were still the decisive weapon at sea and an unshakeable conviction that the Combined Fleet would take the United States forces by surprise. Both assumptions were proved shatteringly incorrect and the Japanese paid a high price for their folly. That the Combined Fleet failed to recover the initiative, once the operation started to break down, was largely due to its complicated plan of deployment. In attempting to cover the transports and carriers in the Aleutians and at Midway simultaneously, Yamamoto dispersed the Combined Fleet over a vast area. Instead of concentrating their strength ready for the decisive encounter with the US Pacific Fleet, the Japanese went into battle with Nagumo's carriers some 300 miles distant from Yamamoto's battleships in the north, and with the ships of the Close Support Group and the Invasion Force separated from each other in the south. When the carriers were attacked the anti-aircraft firepower of Yamamoto's ships was not available to defend them. Though Yamamoto always stressed that the main purpose of the attack on Midway was the destruction of the Pacific Fleet, the greater part of the offensive capability of all four of Nagumo's carriers, at what later transpired to have been the critical moment of the battle, was firmly locked into supporting the invasion. The tactical flexibility so essential to the effective employment of carriers had been fatally compromised. The American conduct of the battle was not without error, and as the action developed the staff work on Spruance's carriers left a great deal to be desired. The compact deployment and handling of the US task forces, however, made recovery from failure quicker and more direct than in the dispersed Combined Fleet.

While the Battle of Midway was being fought to a conclusion, operations in the Aleutians were proceeding amidst some uncertainty, particularly on the part of the US. The Japanese had succeeded in occupying the bare and unpopulated Islands of Attu and Kiska and had repeated their raid on Dutch Harbor. The ill-coordinated forces of the Alaskan Command, under Major General Simon Bolivar Buckner, and the North Pacific Area, under Rear Admiral Robert Theobald, remained largely passive in the face of the Japanese attack and failed to impede the enemy's progress. Once the Japanese landings on Attu and Kiska had been discovered, however, Theobald and Buckner argued strongly for a counteroffensive, but Washington correctly gauged that the occupation force, if left alone for the time being, posed little threat to anyone.

The failure of the Combined Fleet at Midway presented the United States with an opportunity to embark on a limited offensive in the southwest Pacific, where the Japanese threat to the line of communication between the United States and Australia was still very real. General MacArthur proposed that an amphibious force should land an infantry division on New Britain to take the major Japanese staging post at Rabaul. Admiral King, conscious of the grave risk to his carriers inherent in such an operation, countered with a plan for a step-by-step approach to Rabaul through the Solomon Islands. This would accord with the strategic concepts of RAINBOW-5 and would not, it was hoped, further prejudice the deployment of troops in Europe. The capture of Rabaul would also open the way for an eventual Allied advance across the central Pacific to the Philippines and Japan itself. The drawback to King's plan was that at each stage of a grad-

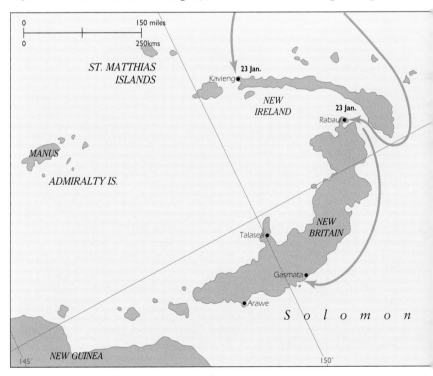

ual advance the assault force would be subjected to attack by Japanese air power at Rabaul. Moreover, costly operations would have to be mounted against enemy positions which would wither on the vine if Rabaul were seized by a bold stroke at the outset.

Although the army and the navy finally agreed on the step-by-step strategy, a bitter dispute raged between King and MacArthur as to who should command the operations. Geographically, command responsibility lay with MacArthur since the actual landings would take place almost entirely within his Southwest Pacific Area. King, who was not inclined to entrust his carriers to MacArthur's command, insisted that as the operations would depend almost completely on navy resources, a sailor, in this case Admiral Nimitz, should be in overall control. The argument was eventually resolved through a compromise proposed by General Marshall. The coming operations would be divided into three phases. The first phase, the occupation of the Santa Cruz Islands and Tulagi, would be under the command of Nimitz. In this phase the boundary between the Southwest Pacific Area and the South Pacific Area would be moved to the west by 1° (to longitude 159° east), thus bringing the southern Solomons within the control of the South Pacific. The second phase, the occupation of the remainder of the Solomons, Papua, and the northeast coast of New Guinea as far as Salamaua and Lae, and the third phase, the attack on Rabaul, would be under MacArthur's command. The Joint Chiefs of Staff imposed their own final authority on the resources to be employed, on when command would pass from Nimitz to MacArthur, and on the timing of the three phases. Phase one (Operation WATCHTOWER) would commence on 1 August 1942. Before WATCHTOWER could be executed, however, the Japanese launched their own offensive in the southwest Pacific.

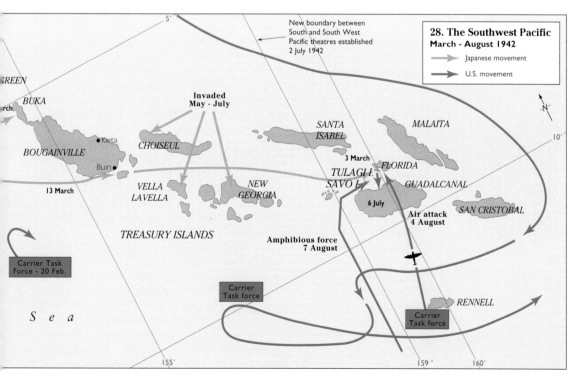

28. The Southwest Pacific March - August 1942

Japanese movement

U.S. movement

New boundary between South and South West Pacific theatres established 2 July 1942

GREEN

BUKA

Invaded May - July

SANTA ISABEL

MALAITA

Kieta

CHOISEUL

BOUGAINVILLE

Buin

3 March

FLORIDA

TULAGI I.

SAVO I.

GUADALCANAL

VELLA LAVELLA

NEW GEORGIA

6 July

SAN CRISTOBAL

13 March

Air attack 4 August

TREASURY ISLANDS

Amphibious force 7 August

Carrier Task Force - 20 Feb.

RENNELL

Sea

Carrier Task force

Carrier Task force

155°

159°

160°

5 The Allied Offensive: New Guinea and the Solomons

Despite the setback to their plans inflicted at the battles of the Coral Sea and Midway, the Japanese were determined to resume the offensive against Port Moresby on the southern coast of New Guinea, and consolidate their position in the Solomons. As the campaigns in the Philippines and the Dutch East Indies drew to a successful close, Imperial General Headquarters was able to transfer men and equipment to the southeast area (as it was from the Japanese view point). In May 1942 a new formation, the 17th Army, under Lieutenant General Harukichi Hyakutake, began to assemble at Palau, Rabaul and Truk, and the Japanese advance through the Solomons reached Tulagi close to the southern end of the island chain. In July the recently created 8th Fleet assumed responsibility for the southeast area, a new Commander-in-Chief, Vice Admiral Gun'ichi Mikawa, arrived in New Britain, and the 25th Air Flotilla at Rabaul was reinforced. This activity was inspired by the need to cut the line of communication between the United States and Australia.

On 21 July, while American preparations for a step-by-step advance through the Solomons were in progress, the Japanese landed 2,000 troops on the north coast of New Guinea. They came ashore close to Buna and Gona, between their own enclaves at Lae and Salamaua and the Australian garrison at Milne Bay. Their objective was a jungle track which ascended the foothills of the Owen Stanley Ranges to Kokoda, a village at 1,200 feet above sea level. From there the track wound up and down through thick bush and across knife-edged ridges to 7,000 feet, before falling to the southern coast and Port Moresby. The Japanese had been stopped from launching an amphibious assault on Port Moresby at the Battle of the Coral Sea, and they were now attempting to take it by the overland route. The Australian command believed that it would be impossible for a substantial force to cover the 100 miles across the mountains using a trail that was at best only two to three feet wide. Conditions on the Kokoda Trail were appalling, and alternated between the harsh, flesh-tearing rock of ridges and spurs, and the putrefaction of a jungle that flowed with black mud. Everywhere there was water; rushing through mountain gorges as near-impassable streams or falling in an incessant storm from the skies. Re-supply was a nightmare for every item of food and ammunition had to be man-handled along the track or dropped by air. Nevertheless, enemy infantry and engineers quickly began to drive the advanced elements of the Australian 39th Militia Battalion and the Papuan Infantry Battalion back along the trail. By 29 July the Japanese had reached Kokoda.

In August General MacArthur rushed reinforcements, in the form of the 7th Australian Division, to New Guinea. The garrison of Port Moresby was strengthened by the arrival of the 21st Australian Brigade (to be followed in September by the 25th Brigade) and the defence of Milne Bay by the 18th Brigade. These veteran troops, under the overall command of Lieutenant General Sir Sydney Rowell, were given the task of retaking Kokoda and pushing the Japanese back to the north coast. This was a difficult proposition since by 21 August there were some 13,500 Japanese troops under Major General Tomitaro Horii fighting their way towards Port Moresby. The

Australians repulsed a sequence of suicide attacks on their positions at Isurava, but slowly sheer weight of numbers began to tell and the Japanese gained ground on the flanks. As their casualties mounted the Australians were forced to abandon their defence perimeter and retire to Ioribaiwa. They did not, however, abandon their wounded who were carried back down the trail by their comrades and by Papuan natives.

MacArthur's staff at his GHQ in Brisbane, who were largely ignorant of the terrain across which the battle was being fought and who lacked combat experience almost to a man, were gripped by near panic when news arrived of a Japanese landing at Milne Bay on the eastern tip of Papua. During the night of 25–26 August some 1,200 Japanese troops, supported by two cruisers and three destroyers, came ashore and attempted to press inland using flanking attacks. This was the second stage of the Japanese offensive against Port Moresby. It was designed to protect the flank of the Kokoda attack and to provide a staging post for amphibious operations against the southern coast of New Guinea. Allied forces had been developing Milne Bay as a forward airbase since June 1942, and by the end of August it had a garrison of nearly 9,000 troops. These were composed of some 7,500 Australian infantry and artillery men and 1,300 Americans in engineer and artillery units. They were supported by 75 and 76 Squadrons of the Royal Australian Air Force (RAAF) flying Kittyhawk fighters.

The Allied base was contained between the mountains and the sea, and within a strip of jungle and swamp which in places was only a few hundred yards wide and never more than two miles in depth. As a result the fighting for Milne Bay was both bloody and confused and the Japanese had the advantage not only of being reinforced but also of deploying tanks. The Australian 7th and 18th Infantry Brigades, with the valiant support of the RAAF which shot up both enemy troop concentrations and shipping, first absorbed the enemy attacks and then fought their way into the Japanese positions. By 6 September Milne Bay was firmly in Allied hands again and mopping up operations were quickly concluded. For the first time in the Pacific War a Japanese beachhead had been thrown back into the sea, and this decisive defeat raised morale of Allied troops throughout the Far East.

On the Kokoda Trail, however, the Japanese were far from finished. The Australians, with many of their troops suffering from malaria and dysentery,

An Australian artillery unit pulling a 25-pounder gun over the difficult terrain of the New Guinea jungle. Australian troops quickly built a reputation for tenacity and resolution in operating in the tough physical conditions of the southwest Pacific.

were outnumbered at the front by almost five to one and although fighting desperately they were forced to pull back from Ioribaiwa to the Imita Ridge. MacArthur, fuming at what he considered Australian military incompetence, dispatched General Sir Thomas Blamey to assume command in New Guinea on 15 September. Blamey sacked General Rowell, replacing him with Lieutenant General Sir Edmund Herring, but changes in command were remote and almost irrelevant to the men fighting on the Kokoda Trail. The trail was the province of the 'poor bloody infantry', soaked to the skin, racked with disease and fever, and thrown into hand-to-hand combat after an exhausting climb to the mountain peaks. The Japanese too were suffering. Their supply position was in chaos, their troops were starving, and ammunition was low. They had sustained nearly 3,000 battle casualties and, with the US Marines fighting their way across Guadalcanal there was no hope of further reinforcements. General Horii was now barely thirty miles from Port Moresby, but on 26 September he received orders to withdraw. Fighting suicide rearguard actions the Japanese pulled back down the trail, leaving, along the way, stark evidence of their savagery towards Australian prisoners and the Papuan natives. Kokoda was retaken by the Australians on 2 November 1942, before the American reinforcements (126th and 128th Regiments) that MacArthur had sent to New Guinea could come into action. After four months of bitter fighting, and at a cost of nearly 1,700

A US anti-aircraft gun camouflaged in an emplacement in New Guinea. With good accuracy and a high rate of fire such guns inflicted significant losses on Japanese aircraft and were also able to disrupt enemy bombing patterns.

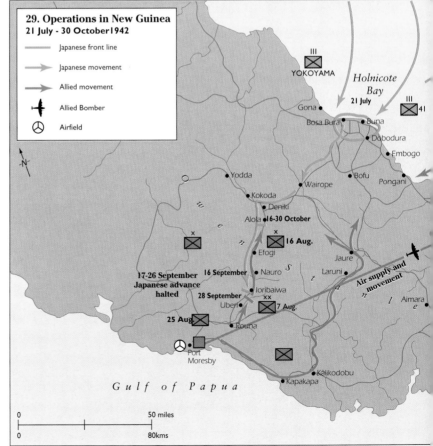

29. Operations in New Guinea
21 July - 30 October 1942

—————— Japanese front line

⟶ Japanese movement

⟶ Allied movement

✈ Allied Bomber

Ⓧ Airfield

Australians killed and wounded, Port Moresby had been saved.

With Kokoda firmly in their hands the Allies began operations to destroy the Japanese enclaves on the north coast of Papua New Guinea at Buna and Gona. The Australian 16th and 25th Brigades (7th Division) attacked along the Kokoda Trail while a battalion from the American 126th Regiment (32nd Division) completed its advance along the Kapa Kapa Trail to the southeast of Kokoda. Exploiting the airstrip constructed at Wanigela, one hundred miles to the northeast of Milne Bay, Australian and American (128th Regiment) troops were moved forward by air and then by small boat to Pongani on the coast south of Buna. With the 16th and 25th Brigades attacking Sanananda and Gona respectively, and part of the 32nd US Division advancing from the south on Buna and Cape Endaiadere, the net was closing around the Japanese. They were to prove, as always, tenacious in defence. With some 9,000 troops deployed around the enclaves in heavily fortified positions, Lieutenant General Adachi was able to make the Allies pay dearly for every foot of ground. Individual strongpoints had to be obliterated and their defenders annihilated before Allied troops could advance to the next enemy position. It was only when tanks and artillery joined the attack that the assault on the villages gained momentum, but even then casualties remained high. On 9 December the Australians, now reinforced by the 21st Brigade, overcame the last Japanese resistance at

In the final assault on Buna, New Guinea, Australian troops with an M3 Stewart light tank destroy pill boxes, while a 2-inch mortar fires on Japanese troops as they flee from their defences.

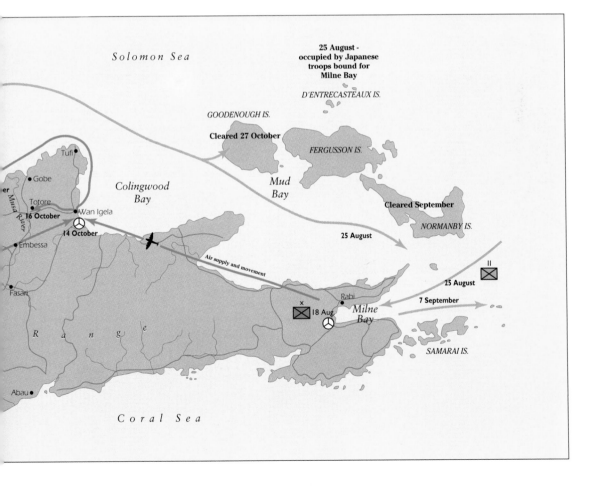

Gona, and they were then able to switch the 18th Brigade and two troops of General Stuart tanks from the 2nd Battalion 16th Armoured Regiment to join the American attack on Buna.

The American advance had not been fast enough for General MacArthur, and Major General Edwin Harding, who led the 32nd US Division during the early attacks on Buna in November, was relieved of his command by Lieutenant General Robert Eichelberger. With their supply position considerably improved by the construction of an airfield at Dobodura, only some eight miles south of Buna, the Allies were finally able to break through the last of the enemy's defences. Their success was facilitated by the fact that the Japanese troops were close to starvation and short of ammunition, and Buna fell on 2 January. The Australian 18th Brigade, the 127th US Regiment, and the 163rd US Regiment (41st Division) cleared the final Japanese resistance along the coastal strip and at Sanananda. By 22 January 1943, after six months of some of the most difficult campaigning of the war and at the cost of 2,900 American and 5,700 Australian casualties, the Japanese thrust in Papua had been eliminated. For the first time in World War II a Japanese land operation had been defeated, even though the Allied forces had been outnumbered for much of the Campaign. Throughout, Australian and American aircraft had played a vital part in supporting front-line units, dropping everything from food and ammunition – missions described as 'biscuits bombers' by the troops – to bridging equipment. This use of air power to provide the logistic support for an overland advance in difficult terrain was to become a particular strength of Allied warfare in the Far East and Pacific theatres. Australian techniques of jungle warfare and tactical leadership, developed during the fighting in Papua, were to be adopted with success by British forces in their campaign in Burma.

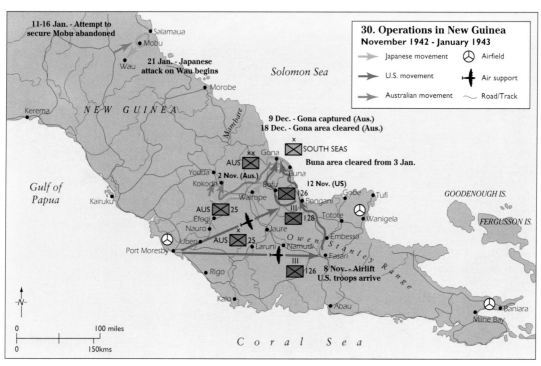

30. Operations in New Guinea
November 1942 - January 1943

On the morning of 7 August 1942 the first phase of the American offensive against the Solomons had begun with a landing by the 1st Marine Division on Guadalcanal and at Tulagi. For the operation, which was under the overall command of Admiral R L Ghormley Commander-in-Chief South Pacific Area, the navy deployed a task force under Rear Admiral Fletcher and an amphibious force under Rear Admiral Richmond K Turner. Altogether

A PBY Catalina Navy flying boat patrols over the Alaskan Peninsula. The Catalina was used extensively in the Pacific for maritime reconnaissance and could carry up to 2,000 pounds of bombs.

eighty-two ships, including three carriers — *Enterprise*, *Saratoga* and *Wasp* – the battleship USS *North Carolina*, thirteen cruisers and thirty destroyers, approached Guadalcanal undetected and put Major General Archer Vandegrift's marines ashore near Lunga Point and on Tulagi. On Guadalcanal (known to the Allies by the code name CACTUS) approximately 2,000 Japanese troops and construction workers had been building the airstrip which was later to become famous as Henderson Field. When the American and Australian warships opened fire the Japanese fled into the jungle and the only resistance encountered was from the garrison on Tulagi and the nearby Islands of Tanambogo and Gavutu.

The first major Japanese reaction came from the air, with attacks by bombers on the transports and their escorts during 7 and 8 August. The bombers, from the 25th Air Flotilla at Rabaul, had been spotted during their approach by an Australian coast watcher in Bougainville who alerted the Americans. As a result either Fletcher's fighters or his guns were waiting for the Japanese planes and the fleet escaped any serious damage. Throughout the Solomons and other campaigns in the South Pacific the coast-watchers, Australian civil servants and planters who remained hidden behind Japanese lines equipped with a radio, were to play a brave and invaluable role in supplying information on enemy movements. Even so, Fletcher regarded the risk of air attack as so grave that on the afternoon of 8 August he announced his intention to carry out the planned withdrawal of the American carriers, plus the *North Carolina*, six cruisers and sixteen destroyers, to a position 100 miles to the southwest of Guadalcanal. Since there had been no warnings of approaching Japanese naval forces from the reconnaissance planes and bombers of MacArthur's Army Airforce squadrons or the naval aircraft of the South Pacific Command, Fletcher assumed that the marines and their transports were in no immediate danger. In fact, a Japanese surface force was on route to Guadalcanal as Fletcher's ships steamed away.

Liaison between Fletcher and Rear Admiral John McCain who commanded 300 land-based naval aircraft and Army bombers left something to be desired. Although bad weather forced McCain to limit his reconnaissance flights during the afternoon of 8 August he failed to inform Fletcher of this problem. As a result the gaps in the reconnaissance screen had not been filled by aircraft from the carriers. Within hours of the American landings on Guadalcanal, Vice Admiral Mikawa had left Rabaul with a task force of five heavy cruisers, two light cruisers and a destroyer. His intention was to launch a surprise night attack on the invasion fleet, but first his ships had to safely negotiate the 600 miles to Guadalcanal. Mikawa was spotted by an RAAF Hudson on the morning of 8 August and later the same day his progress south was reported by an Australian coast-watcher on Vella Lavella Island. Limited reports of this intelligence were poorly distributed amongst the American command and both Admiral Turner, and Rear Admiral V Crutchley VC commanding the ANZAC Squadron, were unaware of Mikawa's true strength, his intentions and the imminence of his arrival.

To reach the transports supporting the landing on Guadalcanal Mikawa's ships would have to sail down the passage, known as the 'Slot', through the Solomon's group of islands. Before entering Iron Bottom Sound, between Guadalcanal and Tulagi, where Turner's ships were assembled, the Japanese would have to swing to the north or south of Savo Island which lay across the southern end of the Slot. While Crutchley left in the cruiser HMAS *Australia* to confer with Turner in Lunga Roads, the Allied covering force patrolled the channels round Savo Island to intercept any night attack on the invasion fleet. The cruisers HMAS *Canberra* and USS *Chicago*, together with two United States destroyers, were deployed to the south of Savo Island, and the cruisers USS *Astoria*, *Quincy*, and *Vincennes*, also with two destroyers, to the north. An advance radar picket was provided to the northwest of Savo by the destroyers USS *Blue* and *Ralph Talbot*. The waters of the sound itself were patrolled by two light cruisers under Rear Admiral Norman Scott.

As Mikawa's ships approached Savo Island they slipped past the USS *Blue*, whose radar was malfunctioning, and took the southern group of Allied warships by surprise. At 1.36 am on 9 August Mikawa launched torpedoes and opened a deadly barrage of gunfire against the Allied cruisers. The Japanese had trained assiduously in the problems of night action between surface fleets, and in their 23-inch oxygen torpedoes, which could deliver 770 pounds of explosive to a range of nine miles at a speed of forty-five knots, they had a weapon that American cruisers simply could not match because most were not equipped with torpedo tubes. The *Canberra* was struck by two torpedoes and battered into a flaming wreck by gunfire, while the *Chicago* was damaged, though not seriously, by a single torpedo. Swinging north towards Tulagi, Mikawa bore down on the second group of Allied cruisers who, despite the mayhem that had just been unleashed to the south of Savo, were still unaware of the presence of the Japanese fleet. As the Japanese searchlights suddenly illuminated the American ships, another terrible volley of gunfire and torpedoes was unleashed. Within minutes the *Astoria*, *Quincy*, and *Vincennes*, who barely had a chance to reply to the enemy bombardment, were reduced to exploding, sinking hulks.

It was a signal defeat which might have been immeasurably worse had Mikawa pressed on southwards to confront the almost defenceless transports and their destroyer screen. Much of the marines' heavy equipment and ammunition had still to be unloaded, and the destruction of Turner's amphibious force would have placed the Solomons operation in extreme jeopardy. Instead, content with his tally of four enemy cruisers sunk or sinking and two destroyers and one cruiser damaged, Mikawa ordered his ships to withdraw northwards up the Slot. The action had only lasted for thirty minutes but Mikawa was concerned that his ships had already expended all their torpedoes, and that, if he lingered, he would be subjected to an attack at dawn by planes from Fletcher's carriers, which the Japanese believed to be still off Guadalcanal. Mikawa's fleet lost no more than a single destroyer during the Battle of Savo Island, but on the return voyage the heavy cruiser *Kako* was sunk by the American submarine *S-44* off Kavieng in New Ireland. Although his covering force had been almost annihilated, and nearly 2,000 Allied sailors killed or wounded, Turner took the commendable decision to continue unloading, only withdrawing his amphibious force in the afternoon of 9 August. For the next two weeks, the 17,000 Marines on Guadalcanal and Tulagi, deprived of naval support and with only one month's rations and four day's ammunition, were virtually isolated. Fortunately the Japanese Army, misled by the navy as to the real import of the Battle of Midway and preoccupied with the campaign in New Guinea, was slow to react to the American landings which it had initially dismissed as merely a reconnaissance in force.

On 13 August General Hyakutake's 17th Army was ordered not only to redouble its efforts to take Port Moresby but also to mount an expedition against Guadalcanal. Believing the American strength on the Island to be no more than 2,000 Marines, Hyakutake allocated only 6,000 men to the task of pushing them into the sea. He also split his forces, landing an advance body of 1,000 troops from the Ichiki Detachment some twenty miles to the east of Henderson Field at Taivu on 18 August, and 500 men of the Special Naval Landing Force seven miles to the west of the Americans at Kokumbona. Before the Japanese main body could arrive on Guadalcanal the troops of the Ichiki Detachment launched a frontal assault on the marines at the Ilu River and were all but wiped out. In order to cover the reinforcement convoy for Guadalcanal, Admiral Yamamoto formed two carrier task forces under Vice Admiral Nobutake Kondo. These were built around the light carrier *Ryujo* and the fleet carriers *Shokaku* and *Zuikaku*, with the *Ryujo* acting as a decoy during its planned attack on Henderson Field. Alerted to the Japanese fleet movements by intelligence intercepts and reports from coast watchers, Admiral Ghormley ordered Fletcher to bring his carriers forward to catch the enemy task forces as they approached the Lower Solomons. Fletcher had the carriers *Enterprise*, *Saratoga*, and *Wasp* under command as well as the battleship *North Carolina*, but he mistakenly believed that the nearest Japanese carriers were still at Truk. He therefore felt able to satisfy his obsession with the fuel stocks of his ships and detach the *Wasp* southwards to oil.

While Fletcher was thus deprived of one third of his strength his search planes spotted the *Ryujo* off Santa Isabella Island on 24 August. An air strike by thirty American dive bombers and eight torpedo planes left the *Ryujo* ablaze and sinking, and Fletcher's defences coped well with the counter-strike launched from the *Shokaku* and *Zuikaku*. The *Enterprise* was hit by three bombs but the *Saratoga* emerged unscathed and American aircraft losses were only seventeen compared to ninety for the Japanese. Both Fletcher and Kondo now withdrew, the latter leaving the transports under Rear Admiral Raizo Tanaka to press on to Guadalcanal alone. However, at dawn on 25 August, B-17s of the Army Air Force, based on Espiritu Santo, and Navy bombers from Henderson, scored a number of hits on Tanaka's ships and persuaded him to turn back. Tactically, the Battle of the Eastern Solomons had been inconclusive, but the Japanese attempt to reinforce their troops on Guadalcanal had been frustrated for the moment. It was now clear that the Japanese had decided to fight hard for the Solomons and both Ghormley and King pressed Marshall for air and ground reinforcements. There were already over 350 bombers and 800 fighters facing 300 Japanese aircraft in the south and southwest Pacific and Marshall refused to increase this figure. Troops were available and, in view of the crisis in New Guinea and the Solomons, the movement of the 43rd US Division to New Zealand and Espiritu Santo was set in train. King, MacArthur, and Ghormley were not satisfied with this response and the argument over competing priorities between Europe, north Africa, and the Pacific was to continue to rumble through the American command structure.

The Japanese withdrew troops, ships and planes from China, the Netherlands East Indies, the Philippines and Truk to support the offensive in the Solomons. Reinforcements and supplies were run in to Guadalcanal by Combined Fleet destroyers and cruisers which timed their voyage down the Slot so that they arrived off the island in darkness. Once the troops and equipment had been landed the Japanese warships would pause to shell the marine's positions and Henderson Field, before returning through the Slot at high speed. So regular were these missions that the marines christened the ships commanded by Rear Admiral Tanaka the 'Tokyo Express'. By September 1942 the recapture of Guadalcanal had become the first priority for Japanese forces in the southeast Pacific, and they were able to bring in some 6,000 reinforcements via the 'Tokyo Express'. Their first successes came at sea, however, with the torpedoing of the *Saratoga* by the submarine *I-26* on 31 August, and a torpedo attack by *I-119* on the *Wasp*, the battleship *North Carolina*, and the destroyer *O'Brien* on 15 September. The *Wasp* sank but the *Saratoga* and the *North Carolina* were able to make harbour for repairs. Admiral Fletcher, who had been slightly wounded in the attack on the *Saratoga*, returned to the United States and eventual banishment to the North Pacific Command for the remainder of the war. Admiral Ghormley was now reduced to one operational carrier, the *Hornet*, with which to support the marines in the Solomons.

On Guadalcanal itself, the Japanese had expended much of their strength in a frontal assault on the aptly named 'Bloody Ridge' on the night of 13 September. Over 50 per cent of Major General Kiyotake Kawaguchi's attacking force had been killed or wounded by the defending marines, who had lost 20 per cent of their own strength. During the next weeks the US Navy ferried in reinforcements, the 7th Marine Regiment, with 4,000 men, landing on Guadalcanal from Samoa on 14 September, while on 9th October the 164th Regiment of the US Army's American Division sailed for the island from New Caledonia. The covering force for this movement included the *Hornet* and the new battleship USS *Washington*, together with a squadron of four cruisers and five destroyers under Admiral Scott. In an attempt to intercept the 'Tokyo Express' Scott deployed his cruisers – *Boise*, *Helena*, *Salt Lake City*, and *San Francisco* – between Cape Esperance and Savo Island on the night of 11–12 October. At 11.30 pm the *Helena* detected five unidentified ships on her radar. These proved to be the Japanese heavy cruisers *Aoba*, *Kinugasa*, and *Furutaka*, with two destroyers, under the command of Vice Admiral Aritomo Goto. The Japanese were taken by surprise and in a confused night action, during which both sides believed for a time that they were firing on friendly ships, Goto was killed, the cruiser *Furutaka* and the destroyer *Shirakumo* sunk, and the *Aoba* damaged. Despite Scott's timely intervention, during which the destroyer *Duncan* was sunk and the cruiser *Boise* badly damaged, the Japanese succeeded in landing their reinforcements on Guadalcanal.

The ace in the American hand was Henderson Field which had been operational since 20 August. Whatever the Japanese Navy might attempt at night, daylight brought US fighters and bombers into the air over Guadalcanal and American dominance of the waters around the island was reasserted. The pilots of Brigadier General Roy Geiger's 'Cactus Air Force' operated under appalling conditions at Henderson, which was regularly subjected to bombing and strafing raids, harassing artillery fire, and bombardment by Japanese cruisers and battleships. In the period of one and a half hours on the night of 13–14 October, for example, the battleships *Haruna* and *Kongo* fired a total of 900 14-inch shells onto the airstrip, destroying aircraft, ammunition, fuel, and installations, as well as providing the American airmen and marines with an experience they would never forget. Notwithstanding such enemy interference Henderson Field maintained its operational capability, though at a fearful cost in pilots and planes.

By the middle of October the Japanese had concentrated some 20,000 troops under General Hyakutake's immediate command on Guadalcanal, and a major portion of the Combined Fleet, including five battleships, five carriers, and fourteen cruisers, were now stationed off the Shortland Islands. It was obvious that a Japanese offensive was imminent. The man who would have to defeat it was Vice Admiral William Halsey, the new Commander-in-Chief of the South Pacific Area, after an exhausted Ghormley

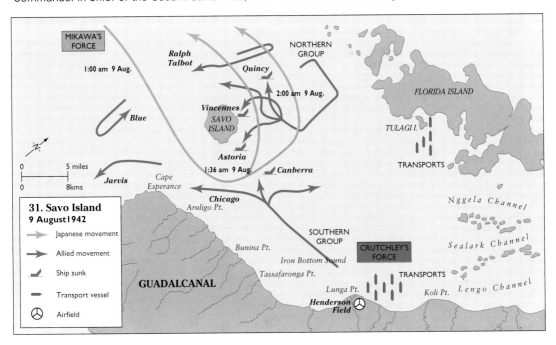

31. Savo Island
9 August 1942

→ Japanese movement
→ Allied movement
↙ Ship sunk
— Transport vessel
⊕ Airfield

had been relieved by Nimitz on 18 October. The Japanese planned to capture Henderson Field using the troops of the 2nd Division under Lieutenant General Masai Maruyama in an attack from the south, while a diversion was launched from the west by a force commanded by Major General Tadashi Sumiyoshi. The Combined Fleet would stand poised to intercept any American reinforcements or surface units making for the Island.

To reach their start position General Maruyama's troops had to cut their way through the jungle from Kokumbona, and they were delayed by difficult ground conditions made even worse by torrential rain. As a result coordination was lost between the advancing Japanese forces, and Sumiyoshi attacked first and in isolation along the Matanijau River. The marines were waiting and the Japanese diversion was turned back with heavy casualties. Maruyama's attack from the south finally began on the night of 23–24 October and its entire strength fell on the 1st Battalion, 7th Marine Regiment and units of the newly arrived 164th Infantry Regiment. During two nights of desperate fighting the Japanese made some temporary penetrations of the American perimeter, but as their casualties steadily mounted they were forced to abandon the attack and retreat to their enclave in the west of the island.

At sea Vice Admiral Kondo, waiting to the northeast of Guadalcanal with a task force of four battleships and four carriers, was confronted by a dispersed American fleet, under Rear Admiral Thomas Kinkaid, amounting to two battleships, two carriers, nine cruisers, and eighteen destroyers. On 26 October both fleets dispatched aircraft to strike the opposing carriers, and in the subsequent battle off the Santa Cruz Islands, the Japanese sank the *Hornet* and damaged the *Enterprise*, the *South Dakota*, the cruiser *San Juan*, and three destroyers. Kondo's task force was able to retire northwards to Truk without opposition, but two of its carriers, the *Shokaku* and the *Zuiho*, had been put out of action by bomb hits on their decks. Although the Japanese still had two operational carriers in the South Pacific to the American's one, Yamamoto was facing a severe shortage of naval aircraft

US Marine tanks engaged in resisting a Japanese counterattack on Guadalcanal.

and experienced pilots. Following what was by now a familiar pattern, both sides again fed reinforcements into the land battle on Guadalcanal while the opposing navies attempted to ensure that their men and supplies arrived intact, and those of the enemy went to the bottom of the sea.

Between 4 and 12 November the Americans landed two regiments of the 2nd Marine Division and another 6,000 troops from the Americal Division at Lunga Point. The reinforcement convoys were escorted by two naval squadrons, under the respective command of Rear Admiral Daniel Callaghan and Rear Admiral Scott, and covered by a task force based around the *Enterprise* and the battleships *South Dakota* and *Washington*. At the same time the Japanese were attempting to run a convoy of eleven transports carrying the main body of the 38th Division from Rabaul to Tassafaronga. The convoy would be supported by units of the 8th and 2nd Fleets operating to the east and west of the southern Solomons, and by a naval bombardment of Henderson Field. During the nights of 8 and 11 November some 2,000 troops were landed safely on Guadalcanal from destroyers, but Vice Admiral Hirosaki Abe's main covering force was spotted coming down the Slot and on the evening of 12 November. Admirals Callaghan and Scott sortied into Iron Bottom Sound with their combined force of thirteen cruisers and destroyers to meet Abe's two battleships – *Hiei* and *Kirishima* – and their escorts. At 1.24 am on Friday 13 November 1942 the Americans located the Japanese warships just to the south of Savo Island at a range of fourteen miles. As Callaghan's ships were attempting to deploy for battle the Japanese opened fire and in the resulting confused, short-range action the Americans lost the cruisers *Atlanta* and *Juneau* together with four destroyers. On the American side only the destroyer *Fletcher* emerged from the battle without damage and both Admirals Callaghan and Scott were killed. Later in the day attacks by aircraft from Henderson Field, the *Enterprise* and Espiritu Santo finished the battleship *Hiei*, which had to be sunk, and inflicted damage and losses on both the Japanese transports and the cruiser bombardment force.

At dusk on 14 November Admiral Kondo returned with the battleship *Kirishima* and four cruisers to cover the transports and to bombard Henderson Field. He was intercepted by Rear Admiral Willis Lee with the *South Dakota* and *Washington* in Iron Bottom Sound. In one of the few battleship-to-battleship actions of the war the *South Dakota* survived over forty large calibre hits, but the *Kirishima*, struck more than fifty times by the radar controlled fire of the *Washington*, was reduced to a sinking wreck. One Japanese and three American destroyers were also sunk, and next day the remaining enemy transports, which had beached at Tassafaronga, were set ablaze by aircraft from Henderson Field and fire from shore batteries. During the night of 30 November eight destroyers under Admiral Tanaka attempted to deliver supplies to Tassafaronga, but they were intercepted off the coast of Guadalcanal by a task force of five cruisers and six destroyers commanded by Rear Admiral Carleton Wright. In the ensuing *mêlée* Tanaka's destroyers mounted a concerted torpedo attack which left the heavy cruisers *Minneapolis*, *New Orleans*, and *Pensacola* damaged and the *Northampton* sinking. In this engagement, the last night action off Guadalcanal, Tanaka lost only a single destroyer but he was unable to land the desperately needed supplies. The Allies had finally won control of the seas around the southern Solomons.

There were now some 20,000 Japanese troops on Guadalcanal who were close to starvation and who lacked any effective or regular means of supply. This was almost the least of their problems for in January 1943 the US launched a sustained offensive to drive the Japanese off the island once and for all. This battle was fought by the newly formed XIV Corps, commanded by Lieutenant General Alexander Patch, comprising the Americal Division, the 25th Infantry Division and the Headquarters and 6th Marine regiment of the 2nd Marine Division. After four months of dogged resistance on Guadalcanal, General Vandegrift and the 1st Marine Division had been relieved for some well earned rest and recuperation. Faced with inevitable defeat in the southern Solomons, Imperial General Headquarters gave orders for the evacuation of all Japanese troops on Guadalcanal. By 7 February 1943 some 13,000 starving, disease ridden survivors of the Japanese garrison had been withdrawn by sea without the Americans realising what was happening. On 9 February General Patch was able to inform Admiral Halsey that: 'Tokyo Express no longer has terminus on Guadalcanal.'

That the Americans had been able to frustrate the Japanese attempts to sustain their operations on Guadalcanal was due not only to the courage of their officers and men, but also to the excellence of their naval intelligence, the dedication and skill of their pilots, both during reconnaissance and attack, and their increasing professionalism in the use of radar at sea. In an opponent such as Admiral Tanaka the United States came up against a dedicated, thoroughly professional seaman and tactician, and it had required the last ounce of Allied commitment to overcome the Japanese. Although it had taken six months to achieve victory, the successful Allied campaigns in Papua and Guadalcanal had lifted the threat to Australia and the lines of communication, and had wrested the strategic initiative from the Japanese. The cost had been high on both sides. In some of the most desperate sea engagements of World War II the United States Navy had

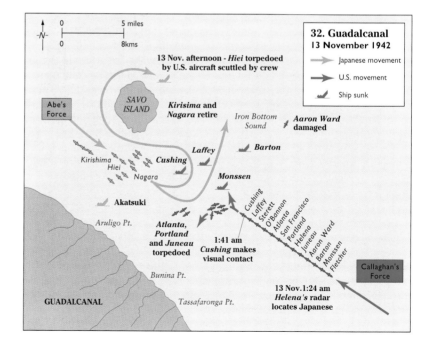

lost two fleet carriers, six heavy cruisers, two light cruisers and fourteen destroyers. The Japanese had also suffered heavily in the waters off Guadalcanal with fleet losses of two battleships, one light carrier, three heavy cruisers, one light cruiser, eleven destroyers and six submarines.

There were many lessons for the United States to learn and areas in which both tactics and technology could be improved. The navy's execution of night actions still left much to be desired, there was as yet no army or navy fighter in the Pacific which could outclass the Zero, and the bombing performance of the B-17 had failed to live up to expectations. Yet for all the difficulties and emergencies, the aura of Japanese invincibility had been shattered in New Guinea and on Guadalcanal. The Allies could now begin to plan an offensive that would eventually destroy the Japanese position in the South Pacific.

By the start of 1943 the strategic picture of the war as a whole was changing. The Allies were no longer purely on the defensive and their armies were pushing back Axis forces on a number of fronts. The British 8th Army, after defeating Rommel at El Alamein, had pursued the *Afrika Korps* across 1,000 miles of north Africa, and the Allied amphibious landings in Algeria and Morocco had penned the Germans in Tunisia. At Stalingrad the Russians had destroyed an entire German Army and their counteroffensive had rolled the Germans back over the River Don. In the Pacific the Allies had finally halted the Japanese southern advance after six months of gruelling combat in Papua and the Solomons.

What remained to be settled was the development of a plan for the defeat of the Axis, the proportion of resources to be allocated to the Far East and to Europe, and a timetable for when offensive action in various theatres would begin. The Anglo-American Conference at Casablanca in January 1943 had produced no final answer to these questions, although it was agreed that while the primary aim was still the defeat of Germany,

US Marines utilising a Japanese gun emplacement on Guadalcanal against its former occupants.

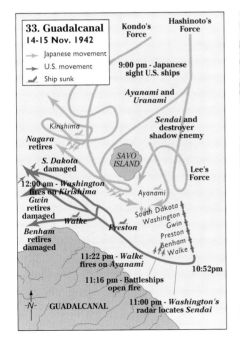

operations aimed at maintaining the initiative against the Japanese could go ahead. In the Pacific this meant the continuation of the Allied offensive against Rabaul; in Burma the mounting of an operation aimed at the recapture of Rangoon; and in Europe the invasion of Sicily and the concentration of troops in Great Britain for an eventual cross-Channel assault. The Japanese meanwhile were concentrating on the defence of Rabaul by holding a line in the central Solomons and New Guinea running from Lae to New Georgia and Santa Isabel.

Before further large scale Allied operations were launched in the Pacific, however, it was vital that the problems encountered in the campaigns in Papua and the southern Solomons should be examined and solutions found. At Guadalcanal the margin of safety had been too narrow. If the Japanese were to be defeated there must be no repetition of a campaign which had staggered from crisis to crisis and which tested Allied resources to the breaking point. The root of the problem lay in the absence of command unity and in the fact that the army and the navy had their own service views of how operations should be conducted. Interservice disputes over the priority to be accorded to airfield construction, over the use of heavy bombers, over the allocation of submarines and surface vessels, and over logistics had made the task of the soldier or sailor fighting the enemy more difficult. There had also been worrying indications of a lack of cooperation between Ghormley's South Pacific and MacArthur's Southwest Pacific Areas. General Marshall attempted to counter the dominance of the service view by appointing naval officers to the staffs of army commanders, and

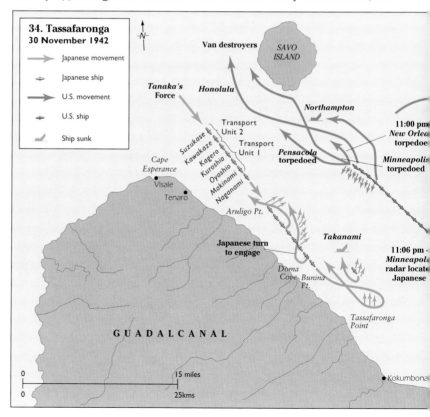

34. Tassafaronga
30 November 1942

→ Japanese movement

⇥ Japanese ship

→ U.S. movement

⇥ U.S. ship

⤸ Ship sunk

-N-

Van destroyers

SAVO ISLAND

Tanaka's Force

Honolulu

Northampton

Transport Unit 2

Transport Unit 1

Pensacola torpedoed

11:00 pm
New Orlea torpedoe

Minneapoli torpedoed

Suzukaze
Kawakaze
Kagero
Kuroshio
Oyashio
Makinami
Naganami

Cape Esperance

•Visale

Tenaro

Aruligo Pt.

Takanami

11:06 pm
Minneapol radar locate Japanese

Japanese turn to engage

Doma Cove Bunina Pt.

Tassafaronga Point

G U A D A L C A N A L

0   15 miles

0   25kms

•Kokumbona

vice versa, but a proposal by General Arnold to reorganise the entire Pacific theatre as a single unified command was not taken up.

Among the lessons underlined by the battle for Guadalcanal and Port Moresby was the vital role that would be played in the Pacific by logistics support. For most of the campaign in the southern Solomons the supply position had ranged from desperate to barely adequate. Lieutenant General Millard Harmon, commanding the US Army Forces in the South Pacific Area, graphically outlined the logistics position in September 1942 in a report to General Marshall:

'Army, navy, and marines all mixed in the jungle, mountains of supplies piling up on the beach, and a road-stead full of ships, bombs, and fuel drums scattered through the coffee and cocoa ...'

At the root of the supply problem lay the acute shortage of shipping available worldwide. But the shortage was compounded by the enormous distances that had to be covered across the Pacific and by a lack of unloading facilities and skilled dock labour. It was estimated that twice as much shipping was required to move a division of troops in the Pacific theatre as in the European. Few docks in the southwest Pacific could handle large cargo ships and in the absence of storage facilities and an effective distribution system, supplies which had reached their destination had to wait on board ship so that the vessel itself became a floating warehouse. With transports

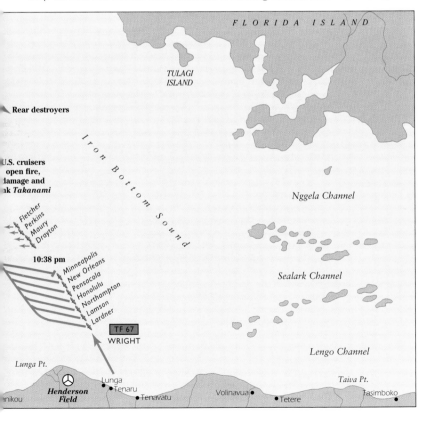

immobilised the shipping crisis could only grow worse. A divided command and the separate requisition systems maintained by the army and navy only amplified the confusion and waste. If the supply position at first proved difficult for the Americans, it increasingly assumed the proportions of a catastrophe for the Japanese. On battlefront after battlefront US air and naval power destroyed the enemy's logistics and Japanese soldiers had to contend not only with Allied attack but increasingly with disease, malnutrition and starvation. Any Japanese unit that ventured far from its base risked destruction, sooner or later, through supply failure.

In the light of the Casablanca conference, and the need to prevent their forces in the Pacific slipping into enforced idleness, the Joint Chiefs decided upon three main operations in the Pacific in 1943. These would be in the south to take Rabaul, in the centre to reach the line Truk-Guam, and in the north to eject the Japanese from the Aleutians. With the completion of Task One, the capture of Guadalcanal and Tulagi in February 1943, the implementation of Tasks Two and Three as set out by the Joint Chiefs' directive of 2 July 1942, could proceed. This involved the occupation of the rest of the Solomons, of the northeast coast of New Guinea, and eventually of New Britain and New Ireland. Admiral King, however, believed that there was a more effective way of prosecuting the campaign against Rabaul; one which would make Tasks Two and Three redundant. Instead of repeating the slow, bloody slog of the fighting on Guadalcanal by again attacking the Japanese defences frontally, why not simply bypass enemy strongpoints by capturing the Admiralty Islands to the northwest of Rabaul? An outflanking

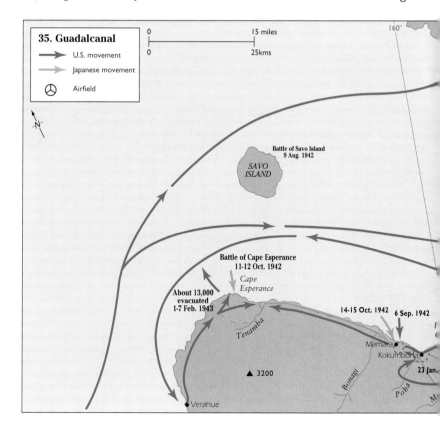

35. Guadalcanal

→ U.S. movement

→ Japanese movement

⊗ Airfield

0   15 miles
0   25kms

160°

Battle of Savo Island
9 Aug. 1942

SAVO
ISLAND

Battle of Cape Esperance
11-12 Oct. 1942

Cape
Esperance

About 13,000
evacuated
1-7 Feb. 1943

14-15 Oct. 1942   6 Sep. 1942

Tenambo

Mamara
Kokumbona

23 Jan.

▲ 3200

Bonagi

Poha

Verahue

operation, rather than a step-by-step attack, would save time and casualties and render the Japanese positions in the Solomons largely impotent. MacArthur rejected King's strategy, because it would have to be executed without land based air support, and submitted his proposal again for phased advances up the Solomons and along the New Guinea coast which would eventually converge on Rabaul.

MacArthur asked for substantial additional forces to carry out his plan, even though in early 1943 there were nearly 375,000 US troops in the Pacific as opposed to 107,000 in Great Britain and 298,000 in the Mediterranean. At the end of March 1943 the Joint Chiefs issued a directive which cancelled that of 2 July 1942, and which set out objectives which were enshrined in a plan known by the code name CARTWHEEL. In the Southwest Pacific Area two regimental combat teams would take Kiriwina and Woodlark in the Trobriand Islands so that airfields could be constructed there. In the next phase five Australian divisions would fight for Lae, Salamaua, Finschafen, Madang, and western New Britain. In the South Pacific Area a US Marine division would seize the Solomons as far north as Bougainville. MacArthur would exercise strategic command while Halsey would be in tactical command in the Solomons. While planning was in progress the battlefronts had not remained static.

Halsey had been the first off the mark with an amphibious assault by the 43rd Division and attached marines on 21 February against the Russell Islands between Guadalcanal and New Georgia. The islands had already been evacuated by the Japanese and their capture was effected without

US troops stacking containers of howitzer shells at an ammunition dump in New Guinea. The overall logistical system of the Allied forces was superior to that of the Japanese and its efficiency became a decisive factor in prosecuting the war in the Far East.

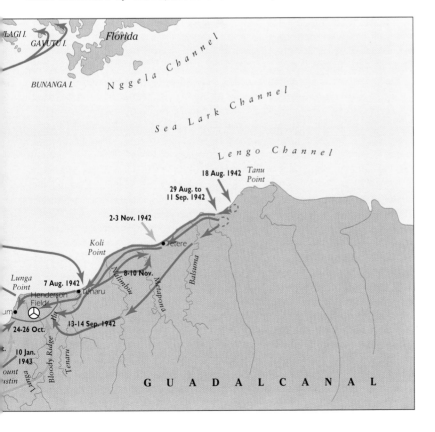

loss. In New Guinea the Australian Kanga Force, defending the village and airfield of Wau, was reinforced by the 17th Australian Brigade which went straight into action as its transport planes landed. Troops of the Japanese 51st Division who had been about to overrun Wau were thrust back to Mubo. Despite this setback the Japanese were determined to support their position in New Guinea for it represented the western hinge of their defensive perimeter in the South Pacific. A convoy of eight transports escorted by eight destroyers sailed from Rabaul at the end of February, carrying 7,000 Japanese troops of the 51st Division and Headquarters 18th Army as reinforcements to Lae. Spotted by reconnaissance planes, the convoy was attacked at low level by American and Australian bombers over two days and lost all the transports and four of the destroyers. It was the birth of Allied land based airpower as a potent weapon in the Pacific, and Lae and Salamaua could now only be supplied by barge or submarine.

In an attempt to gain control of the skies above New Guinea and the Solomons, Admiral Yamamoto launched an air offensive, Operation I-GO, in which the 11th Air Fleet employed some 300 aircraft against Allied forward bases. They were confronted by alert fighter defences which could now deploy planes, such as the twin-engine P-38 Lightning and the Chance-Vought F4U Corsair, with a substantially improved performance over earlier aircraft. Despite the heaviest Japanese raids since Pearl Harbor the damage inflicted on Allied shipping and airpower was slight, and the 11th Air Fleet lost more irreplaceable pilots. The Japanese Navy also lost Admiral Yamamoto. On 18 April 1943, eighteen P-38s, using intelligence information that Yamamoto would be flying to southern Bougainville, pounced on the admiral's fighter escort and shot down his plane over the jungle. Within weeks of the admiral's state funeral in Tokyo on 5 June, the Allied offensive in New Guinea and the central Solomons, which he had attempted to forestall, was launched in all its fury.

The amphibious operations in the Solomons were spearheaded by a new class of specialised vessel, produced at the behest of the British Admiralty, and designed to deliver assault troops and heavy weapons on to enemy held shores. All these vessels had a shallow draught which enabled them, if necessary, to ground on a beach or sand bank where they could discharge their human or equipment cargo straight into action. The largest was the Landing Ship Tank or LST, known to its crews for its lack of speed as 'Large Slow Target', which could deliver tanks, vehicles and troops, or serve as anything from a hospital ship to an ammunition supply depot. There was also a smaller and faster vessel designated Landing Craft Infantry (LCI) which put troops ashore via gangways hinged to the bow. While the LST and LCI were seagoing ships, two small landing craft, the LCT (Landing Craft Tank) and LCVP (Landing Craft Vehicles and Personnel) were normally carried to their destination aboard a mother ship. They were then launched off the enemy beaches and completed the final run ashore under their own power. Truly amphibious vehicles such as the LVT (Landing Vehicle Tracked) and the AMTRAC (Amphibious Tractor) could carry men and supplies from the ocean onto the beach and then forward into the jungle without pause. Such landing vessels gave the initial assault on an enemy shore greater strength, momentum and flexibility, and also contributed to more effective logistical support. The majority of the new landing ships and craft were assigned to Admiral Halsey with a smaller number gradually reaching MacArthur's Amphibious Force, Southwest Pacific.

In June 1942, as part of the Midway operation, Japanese forces had taken the Islands of Attu and Kiska in the Aleutians. The desperate battles at Guadalcanal and in New Guinea had limited the American reaction to the occupation of Adak and Amchitka and the construction of airfields on these islands only some fifty miles from Kiska. The Japanese had been able to deliver some reinforcements to the Aleutians, but on 26 March 1943 a convoy was intercepted off the Komandorskie Islands, and although the American ships suffered the greater damage in the subsequent running fight the Japanese turned back without completing their mission. On 11 May a United States task force comprising an escort carrier and three battleships landed troops of the 7th Division, under Major General Albert Brown, on Attu. The landing was unopposed, but the Japanese, who had concentrated their troops in the mountains, fought to the death before the island was finally taken on 29 May. Kiska was now heavily bombed and on 15 August a task force of 30,000 American troops and 5,000 Canadians went ashore in an amphibious landing. They found the garrison of almost 6,000 men had been successfully, and secretly, evacuated to Japan two weeks earlier. A strategically unimportant, but emotionally significant, group of islands had tied down thousands of Allied troops and hundreds of ships and aircraft that could have been employed more profitably elsewhere.

While events were unfolding in the freezing waters of the north Pacific, operations in the south had begun at the end of June with the occupation of Woodlark and Kiriwina by a brigade from 'Alamo Force' (32nd and 41st US Divisions), and a landing at Nassau Bay, south of Lae, by the 162nd Regiment. At the same time New Guinea Force, drawn from the 3rd, 5th, 7th, 9th, and 11th Australian Divisions plus United States Army regiments, launched an attack on Salamaua. Fighting in exceptionally difficult country the 3rd Australian Division, under Major General S Savige, had driven the Japanese northeast to Mubo, while the 162nd fought its way north along the coast to Tambu Bay only six miles south of Salamaua. By 19 August

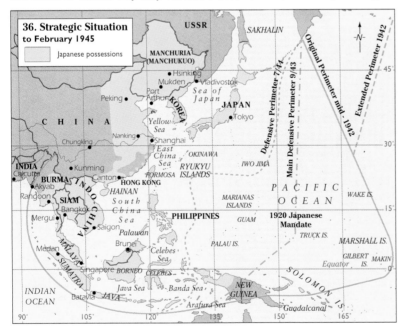

36. Strategic Situation to February 1945

the Japanese were clinging desperately to the outer defences of Salamaua itself, and attacks on individual Japanese positions became mini-battles in their own right. In this bitter fighting the Allied troops drew much of the strength of the Japanese 51st Division to the Salamaua area, thereby facilitating the assault on Lae which began on 4 September.

Salamaua fell to the Australian 29th Infantry Brigade on 16 September, twelve days after an amphibious landing by troops of the 9th Australian Division had been successfully accomplished eighteen miles to the east of Lae. The next day three battalions of the 503rd US Parachute Regiment jumped into Nadzab to the northwest of Lae, and secured the airfield for the arrival of the 7th Australian Division. Lae was now under attack from the east along the Huon Peninsula and from the west along the Markham Valley, and Australian troops entered the town on 15 September. Little was known of the enemy's strength at Finschafen, the next major Japanese base, but the decision was taken to land the 20th Brigade before dawn on 22 September on beaches four miles north of the base. The landing was a success despite fierce opposition and Finschafen was taken on 2 October. The next Allied objective was Sattelberg, but the Australians postponed their intended advance and made preparations to meet a major Japanese attack, the details of which had been obtained through signals intelligence. The Japanese assault, by sea and land, on the Allied beach head was driven off by the US Navy and the 9th Division with heavy enemy losses.

An aerial photograph of ships in Adak Harbor in the Aleutians during the invasion of Kiska in August 1943.

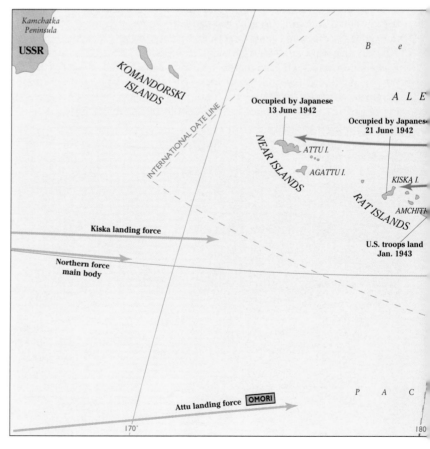

The assault on Sattelberg was quickly resumed and after a hectic period of attack and counterattack the town fell to the Australians on 25 November. The Allies were winning the battle for the Huon Peninsula but the Japanese defence never slackened, and it was only after bitter fighting that the Australians relieved the garrison of Pabu and took Gusika on the coast. Gradually the supremely professional Australian battalions, backed by superior Allied tactics, airpower, and logistics wore the Japanese down. The advance gathered pace despite the appalling terrain that had to be crossed, and the 9th Division entered Sio on 15 January 1944. Inland from the 9th Division their comrades of the 7th Division had been fighting their way down the Markham Valley towards the Finisterre Ranges, and holding the attention of some 12,000 Japanese in the process. During the spring of 1944 the veteran 6th, 7th and 9th Australian Divisions were relieved in New Guinea to form I Corps in Queensland, and they were replaced as New Guinea Force by the II Corps consisting of the 3rd, 5th, and 11th Militia Divisions. This move presaged a change in strategy by which American troops would increasingly take over the operational role of Australian units in New Guinea. The Australians would be used for mopping-up operations to relieve American divisions which had made the initial assaults in the island-hopping campaigns. Even though the surviving enemy units were isolated from their source of supply, they were still armed and thus constituted a threat which had to be contained. It would be the duty of the

Australian troops using flame throwers to clear an enemy position in Borneo.

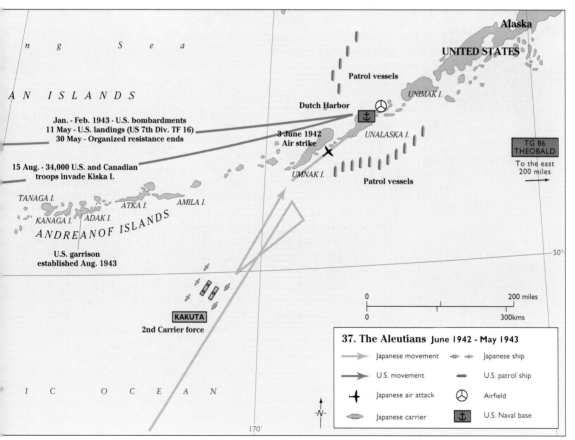

Australian divisions to hunt down and eliminate these Japanese garrisons along the American line of communications. The Australians had shouldered the heaviest burden of the fighting in New Guinea with, for example, 492,000 troops deployed in the southwest Pacific in August 1943 as opposed to 198,000 American troops. Their campaigns during the remainder of the war were largely thankless and unsung, but the Australians continued to uphold their fine reputation and they remained a scourge to the Japanese wherever they found them.

While the assault on the Huon Peninsula was taking place, the offensive in the central Solomons was breaking over New Georgia in the shape of a task force commanded by Admiral Halsey and the 43rd US Division supported by elements of a US Marine Raider regiment and Fijian commandos. The main objective was the airfield at Munda on New Georgia Island which was defended, along with other strategic points, by some 11,000 troops drawn from the Japanese 6th and 38th Divisions and the Kure 6th and Yokosuka 7th Special Naval Landing Forces. Halsey targeted the preliminary landing on Rendova Island which, although separated by seven miles of ocean from New Georgia itself, offered access for large vessels through the coral reefs and a sheltered harbour. Rear Admiral Turner commanding the 3rd Amphibious Force divided the landings into two, with a Western Landing Force to carry out the main assault against Munda Point and an Eastern Landing Force to execute the secondary landings. An intense effort was put into ensuring that adequate logistical and air support was available to the 43rd Division, and secondary landings were made to secure Segi Point (taken on 20 June 1943) for the construction of a fighter airstrip, and Wickham Anchorage (taken on 30 June) as a logistic support area.

Australian troops building an iron roadway across a beach to enable vehicles to come ashore from an American LST.

Rendova was taken against sporadic opposition but from the start the main campaign on New Georgia went badly. The troops of the 43rd Division suffered heavy battle casualties and were sapped of their energy by the swamps, hills and jungle of the island. Two more divisions, the 25th and 39th were rushed in to support the 43rd and Major General Griswold, commanding the XIV US Corps, took control of operations. After a prolonged battering by Allied aircraft, bombardment by warships, and a sustained ground assault, Munda airfield was taken on 5 August and the whole of New Georgia was occupied three weeks later. The Japanese had mounted naval convoys to bring reinforcements into the central Solomons and a number of clashes occurred between opposing warships. The cruiser USS *Helena* was sunk in Kula Gulf, and on 13 July in the Battle of Kolombangara the veteran Japanese light cruiser *Jintsu* was sunk, and one Royal New Zealand Navy cruiser and two American cruisers damaged. While the battle for New Georgia was in progress Admiral Halsey contemplated how to deal with the other Japanese held islands in the group: Arundel, Kolombangara, and Vella Lavella. Assault landings were made on Arundel and Vella Lavella, but Halsey decided to bypass the 11,000 strong garrison on Kolombangara. With the loss of Arundel and Vella Lavella, the latter after tough fighting by the 14th New Zealand Brigade, the Japanese evacuated Kolombangara and Halsey was able to concentrate on his next step, the invasion of Bougainville. Kolombangara was the first example of a deliberate leap-frogging strategy being put into effect and it was soon to become the general policy in the Pacific. Again, an island campaign provided much food for thought among American strategists, particularly in relation to the question of unity of command in joint operations.

6 The Allied Offensive: The Gilbert Islands to Manchuria

As Allied successes steadily mounted the Japanese high command also had a great deal to consider, and in September 1943 Imperial General Headquarters called a conference to review future strategy. With the defeat of Italy, and Germany's increasingly perilous situation in the campaign against Russia, there was obviously little hope of assistance from Europe. Japan would have to fight to the end in the Pacific on her own and the essential commitment of the armed forces must be the defence of the home islands. To sustain this defence, however, it was vital that control of the sources of raw materials captured in the first months of the war, and of the lines of communication needed to transport them to Japan, be retained. It was also starkly apparent that Japan was massively out-classed by the industrial and manufacturing base of the United States, and that it would be impossible to hold the present front line in the southeast Pacific indefinitely. It was therefore decided that an absolute national defence line would be established from Timor, through western New Guinea and the Caroline Islands, to the Kuriles. The commitment to operations in China, and Burma, and to the defence of Manchuria would continue, but the remaining positions in the southeast Pacific would not be further reinforced and would be held purely as a delaying operation. In this way time would be gained for the preparation of the absolute defence line.

While the bitter battles of New Guinea and the Solomons had raged from the summer of 1942 to the winter of 1943, the burden of operations against the Japanese in the central Pacific had fallen on the submarines of the Pacific Fleet. They had discharged this role to some effect, sinking 300,000 tons of Japanese shipping in the four months after Pearl Harbor alone, but plans were already being formulated for an offensive by amphibious forces. The campaign was to take place in Micronesia, an area of the Pacific which contained over 1,000 tiny islands dispersed in four main groups. Advancing from east to west an amphibious assault would first encounter the Gilbert Islands, then the Marshall Islands before reaching the 550 islands of the Caroline group spreading across some 2,000 miles of ocean. Finally came the Mariana Islands stretching 400 miles from Guam to a point only some 500 miles distant from Iwo Jima. In war these island groups controlled the line of communication between the United States and the Philippines and sat across the strategic route to the western Pacific. By the end of 1941 they were all in the hands of the Japanese and together they constituted a vital sector of their defence perimeter. The Islands were of equal importance to the United States since they formed the time-honoured line of advance to the Philippines enshrined in Plan ORANGE during the 1920s and 1930s. The advance was conceived as a step-by-step, fighting approach by the Pacific Fleet with individual islands providing the steps. As one step was occupied it could be converted into a base which would support the next step forward.

At the Casablanca Conference it was evident that Plan ORANGE was once more to see the light of day. There was, however, no attempt to insert ORANGE as a replacement for the campaign underway in New Guinea and the Solomons, and while the battle for Guadalcanal was still being fought there were simply not enough resources to spare for an offensive in the central Pacific. Yet Admiral King raised the salient question of what the Allies would do after the Solomons campaign was over. For most of the navy there was only one answer, recapture the Philippines; and for this there was only one route, the central Pacific. The final report from the conference allowed for advances, 'as practicable' north from Rabaul, northwest from Samoa, and west from Midway. King was forced to bide his time, however, since his Admirals – Nimitz, Halsey, and Spruance – who were already fighting in the South Pacific were opposed to any operation that might divert resources from the Solomon's campaign. MacArthur fully acknowledged the strategic damage that would be inflicted on Japan's war effort by the capture of the Philippines, but he was convinced that the central Pacific approach offered few advantages, particularly to a commander in the South Pacific. He advocated instead an advance via the northern coast of New Guinea and Mindanao, the shortest route and one which would best exploit the strike power of land based aircraft.

The QUADRANT Conference between President Roosevelt, Prime Minister Churchill and their staffs began in Quebec on 14 August 1943, and during its deliberations a central Pacific strategy was authorised. In 1943–44 operations would be mounted to project Allied power from the Gilbert Islands to the Marianas. This massive offensive would also encompass the islands of Ponape, Truk, Palau, Yap, and Guam. At the same time the advance in the southwest Pacific would continue with operations in New Guinea aimed at the eventual capture of the Vogelkop Peninsula at the northwest tip of the island, and with the capture or neutralisation of the Admiralty Islands, the Bismarck Archipelago and Rabaul. The twin thrusts of the central and southwest Pacific campaigns would be mutually supporting, but the central drive would have ultimate priority. It was hoped that by pursuing this strategy it would be possible to divide and destroy the remaining Japanese naval strength, and keep the enemy unsure and off-balance as he attempted to cope with multiple blows of a widely spread offensive.

The first assault in the central Pacific struck the Gilbert Islands in November 1943. Its planning and coordination had been a complex task, for the forces committed to the campaign were out of all proportion to those used previously. At Pearl Harbor the 5th Fleet under Admiral Spruance totalled some nineteen aircraft carriers, twelve battleships and a comprehensive range of cruisers and escort vessels. The logistic support of such a fleet at sea for an extended period was a critical problem, and the solution was found in a floating supply train. This provided oil tankers, ammunition ships, repair ships, tugs, hospital ships, and supply vessels which together represented a floating base that followed the fleet wherever it sailed. The troops that would make the assaults on three atolls of the Gilberts – Abemama, Makin, and Tarawa – were carried by Admiral Turner's 5th Amphibious Force. Nearly 7,000 officers and men of the US Army's 27th Division would strike Butaritari in Makin, while some 18,000 marines of the 2nd Marine Division went ashore on Betio Island in Tarawa. As the assault fleets neared the Gilberts the Japanese Navy was almost powerless to intervene. Ironically, just when an engagement between the Combined Fleet and the Pacific Fleet beckoned, Admiral Mineichi Koga, Yamamoto's successor, had already dispatched nearly 200 of his carrier planes and a force of heavy cruisers south to Rabaul. Without their protection Koga dared not sortie from Truk with his battleships against the 5th

Fleet. He was forced to rely upon interdiction by submarines and aircraft.

In a tactical programme that was to be repeated many times, and with growing violence, across the central Pacific, the landing of units from the 27th Division at Butaritari on 20 November was preceded by air strikes on the defences, by a two hour bombardment by warships of the fire support group, and by rocket and machine gun strafing. The garrison of Butaritari amounted to no more than 800 men but in the confined space of the island it was three days before all resistance had been overcome. The Japanese lost 395 dead while American casualties, including the sailors and airmen killed during the sinking of the escort carrier *Liscome Bay* by the submarine *I-175*, totalled 860. The opposition on Betio, one hundred miles to the south, was considerably stronger with in-depth fortifications that began with log and concrete obstacles on the surrounding reef, continued with more obstacles and barbed wire fences in the water and on the beach, and culminated in bomb-proof bunkers and tunnels. A garrison of 4,800 men was supported by artillery up to 8-inch calibre. On 20 November the marines of the 2nd Division, in one of the most difficult amphibious assaults in history, fought their way across the beaches assisted by Amtracs and Sherman tanks. Once the beach defences had been destroyed the interior of Betio was more lightly held and the marines were able to sweep across the island. By 23 November it was in their hands but at a terrible price. The epithet 'Bloody' Tarawa had been cruelly earned, for with the exception of seventeen wounded soldiers and 129 Korean labourers the Japanese garrison had died to a man. The marines suffered 3,300 casualties. Their commanding officer, General Holland Smith, for one, did not believe that Tarawa's importance was sufficient to justify such carnage.

In the South Pacific the CARTWHEEL offensives were progressing under Halsey and MacArthur's command. Bougainville and its associated islands were garrisoned by approximately 40,000 Japanese troops, and Halsey decided to repeat the tactic he had used at Kolombangara and leap-frog the main areas of Japanese strength. Halsey began his campaign with the capture of the Treasury Islands by the 8th New Zealand Brigade, and with a sustained aerial attack by the 5th USAAF from New Guinea against Rabaul. Aircraft from the South Pacific Area, assisted by cruiser and destroyer bombardment, neutralised all the airfields on southern Bougainville and Shortland Island before the invasion on 1 November 1943. The American landing on the west coast at Torokina took the Japanese by surprise and the near impassable interior of Bougainville meant that they were not able to launch a counterattack until 8 March 1944. By this time the Americal Division, which had relieved the 3rd Marine Division, and the 37th Division had established a formidable defence perimeter despite repeated attempts to destroy the beach-head by Japanese air and naval forces. These attacks were repulsed with heavy losses as was the Japanese 6th Division's assault on the thirteen miles of American perimeter. After two weeks of fighting, and with 5,500 casualties, the 6th Division was ordered to withdraw. Thereafter the Japanese virtually ignored the American presence on the island. Over 37,000 Japanese troops of the 17th Army were now effectively cut off on Bougainville and four Australian Militia Brigades (7th, 11th, 15th, and 29th) began the task of hunting them down in October 1944. After a long and, to some observers, pointless campaign which cost the Australians 2,000 casualties, the surviving 23,500 Japanese on the island surrendered in August 1945.

By the end of 1943 MacArthur's advance in the southwest Pacific, the southern arm of the pincer movement on Rabaul, had reached the Vitiaz Strait, the bottleneck between New Britain and New Guinea. In a two-pronged offensive General Walter Krueger's 'Alamo Force' (US 6th Army) swung east against Cape Gloucester and Arawe in New Britain, while the advance in New Guinea was pushed along the north coast of the Huon Peninsula towards Madang. After fierce fighting in western New Britain the Japanese withdrew to Rabaul in February 1944 and allowed the war to sweep past them towards the Philippines. Although the original aim of CARTWHEEL had been the elimination of the Japanese garrison in Rabaul, it had been decided to by-pass this objective rather than take it. Now that Allied air power was within range of Rabaul the harbour, airfields and installations could be neutralised by fighter and bomber attack, and an amphibious or land assault was unnecessary. From February 1944 the Japanese base at Rabaul remained in being, but in limbo, until the end of the war. Rabaul was part of a tactical pattern that was emerging in Allied operations in the Pacific. Frontal attacks against a strongly fortified island or base would be avoided whenever possible, and Allied assaults would target key areas but avoid Japanese garrisons that were strategically unimportant.

Whatever optimism remained in the ranks of the Japanese high command, the Allied successes in the south and central Pacific during the winter and spring of 1943–1944 brought home the reality of their military position. Japan's armed forces were still strong, particularly on land, and capable of inflicting great damage, but at sea and in the air they were increasingly unable to replace their losses in ships and pilots. The Japanese command discounted the possibility that their own forces could launch any sus-

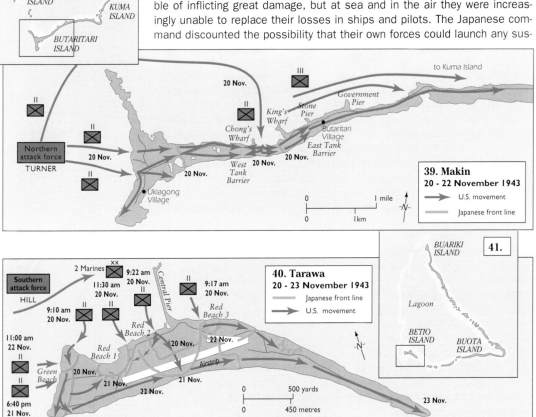

tained counteroffensive before 1946 at the earliest. Moreover, Nimitz's use of carrier task forces to provide air cover for the assault on the Gilberts, had demonstrated that the United States no longer needed to rely upon land based fighter cover for amphibious operations. The Pacific Fleet could now strike anywhere and at almost any distance. Despite these worrying developments in the central Pacific the Japanese were particularly concerned about Allied progress in the South Pacific. They concluded that the enemy's southern thrust was aimed at the seizure of the Philippines and Formosa, and that this was a necessary prelude to an Allied assault upon the home islands. For Imperial General Headquarters the Philippines had become the critical area for the defence of Japan, New Guinea the critical battleground for the approaches to the inner defences of the empire.

Bodies on the beach at Tarawa provide stark evidence of the ferocity and exceptional casualty level of the assault on the island.

While the Japanese pondered the strategic equation the Allies, at the Trident (Washington, May 1943), Quadrant (Quebec, August 1943), and Sextant (Cairo–Tehran, November–December 1943) conferences, had looked in depth at the future outline of operations in the Far East. Winston Churchill and General Sir Claude Auchinleck, Commander-in-Chief in India, believed that British resources could be best applied, strategically, through an amphibious offensive against northern Sumatra or Singapore. The American Joint Chiefs were at first insistent that Great Britain should bend all its efforts to attempting to open road communications with China through the occupation of northern Burma. Auchinleck did not believe that the latter course would be possible during the dry weather of 1943–44 for logistical and administrative reasons, and he argued that the available resources should be applied to increasing the air lift to China. If, at the same time, the line of communication eastwards from Calcutta was

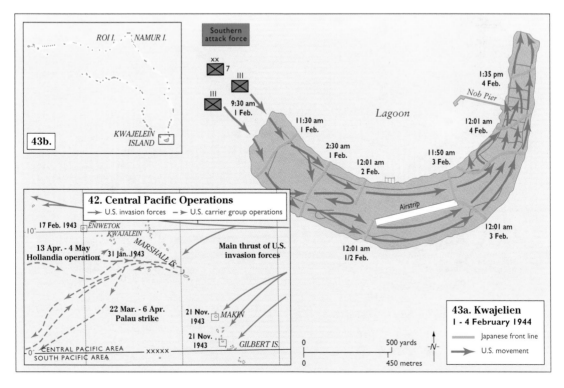

improved then an offensive for the reconquest of Burma might be launched in the dry season of 1944–45. By the time of the Cairo conference the Americans were prepared to agree to a postponement of the offensive in Burma. This had the effect of relegating China to secondary status as a theatre of war and of reinforcing the primacy of the Pacific. Also at Cairo the Allies set out their war aims in the Far East. Japan was to be punished for its aggression and the areas it had occupied returned to their former owners. Korea would be given its independence and Manchuria and Formosa ceded to China. Stalin also pledged, at Tehran, that the Soviet Union would join the war against Japan once Germany had been defeated.

At Cairo the options for bringing about the final defeat of Japan were again debated at some length, with the planners building upon strategic policies considered at Quebec. Three proposals had been put forward: a bombing offensive, an air and sea blockade, and a ground invasion. It was held that Japan would not surrender until the home islands had been invaded and all resistance crushed. At best this would be a difficult and costly undertaking and the preferred option would be to destroy Japan's ability to continue the fight. If possible this would be achieved by blockade and bombing with invasion reserved to a last resort. The most appropriate areas from which to bomb Japan were in eastern China and Formosa, and the preferred route of advance to these bases was the central Pacific. It was thought that these areas would be secured by 1946 and that an invasion, if required, might be possible in 1947. The Combined Chiefs of Staff feared that this timescale would have a dilatory effect on operations, and the conference report declared that the Allies would aim to defeat Japan

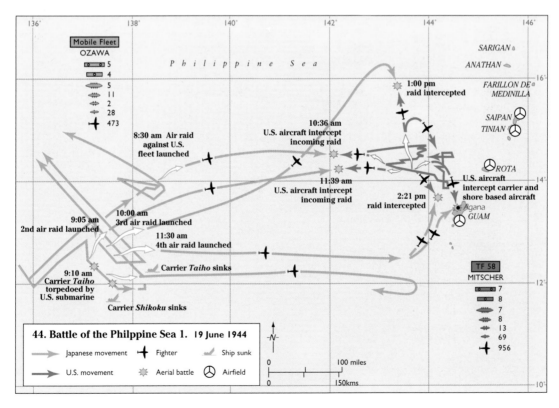

44. Battle of the Philppine Sea 1. 19 June 1944

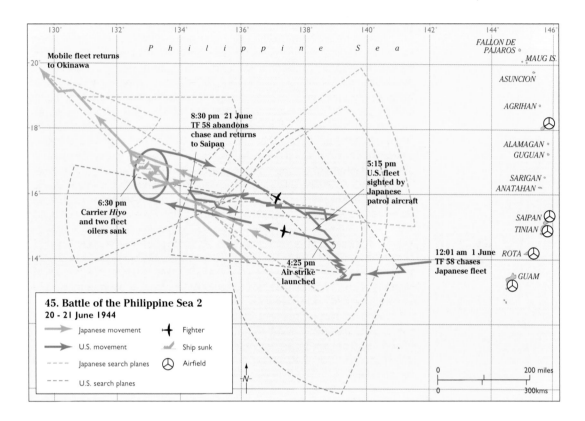

45. Battle of the Philippine Sea 2
20 - 21 June 1944

within one year of the end of hostilities with Germany. An air plan centred around the new B-29 bomber and its 1,500 mile operational range had been submitted at Quebec by General Arnold, and it was on this basis that the more optimistic timetable had been adopted. Arnold's plan envisaged a force of up to twenty groups of B-29s based in the Changsha area of China, and predicted that their bombing offensive would shatter Japanese industry and commerce by the autumn of 1945. As it happened the air plan itself was rejected on logistical grounds. As Rear Admiral Bernard Bieri pointed out in October 1943:

'When the full weight of our air and naval power is deployed against her, we may find the road much easier than anticipated.'

With this in mind the prime objective in the Far East became the acquisition of strategic bases from which an effective and sustained bomber offensive could be launched against Japan. To achieve the sites for these bases the southwest and central Pacific drives would be given priority, and would be aimed at acquiring the Philippines–Formosa–east China triangle. Also with the B-29s in mind, and given the probable logistical problems of operating aircraft from China, the seizure of the Marianas was seen as urgent.

The objectives in 1944 for the central Pacific forces under Admiral Nimitz, as set out by the Cairo Conference, were the capture of the Marshall Islands, Ponape, Truk, and the Mariana Islands. The Marshalls comprise several hundred atolls divided into two almost parallel groups dispersed over a considerable area of ocean. Against the advice of his admirals, Nimitz's major point of attack was Kwajalein Atoll, the command centre of the Marshals and the focus of Japanese air power in the Islands. Landings would be carried out on Namur, Roi, and Kwajalein Islands, and these assaults would be preceded by the occupation of Majuro Atoll, which would serve as a fleet anchorage. Four atolls, Maloelap, Mili, Jaluit, and Wotje, all of which were believed to be strongly garrisoned, would be avoided and by-passed. Their airfields were first pounded by both carrier and land based aircraft, and as the moment of invasion approached battleships and cruisers added the weight of their broadsides to the devastation already inflicted. When the soldiers and marines of Spraunce's 5th Fleet landed on 1 February, there were few Japanese planes left to oppose the invasion. Supported by the main armament of battleships firing from as close as 1,500 yards from the beach, the amphibious assaults first took the islets guarding the entrances to the lagoons, organised them as artillery fire bases, and then stormed ashore on the main islands. The US Army's 7th Division fought its way across Kwajalein Island while, forty miles to the north, the 4th Marine Division attacked Roi and Namur. By 4 February the main Japanese pockets of resistance had been crushed and only weak and isolated garrisons remained to be dealt with.

So swift had been the victory at Kwajalein Atoll that Nimitz ordered Spruance to assault Eniwetok on 17 February, nearly six weeks ahead of schedule. The landings were to be covered by Rear Admiral Marc Mitscher's Fast Carrier Force which would strike the Combined Fleet's base on the island of Truk. Mitscher's pilots destroyed the remaining Japanese air strength in the area, and alongside their own battleships sank most of the shipping that was in the harbour or attempting to escape. The Army's 106th Infantry and the 22nd Marine Regiments landed on Eniwetok undisturbed by enemy air or naval units, and after five days of heavy fighting secured the Atoll. The precision and speed of the seizure of the Marshalls led to a revision of the timetable for American operations in the Pacific in 1944. Nimitz advised the Joint Chiefs of Staff that the assault on the Mariana Islands could be advanced to 15 June 1944, and that Truk could now be neutralised rather than captured. An irresistible form of warfare had come to the Pacific: the fast carrier task force and the all-arms amphibious assault, supported by the most powerful industrial base in the world.

Alarmed at the speed with which the Marshalls had fallen and at the efficiency and violence of the American attack, Imperial General Headquarters began to transfer additional infantry divisions from Manchuria and Japan to the islands forming the absolute defence line. Great reliance was placed upon the capabilities of land based aircraft, and the newly formed 14th Air Fleet joined the 4th Fleet and the 31st Army in Admiral Nagumo's Central Pacific Area Fleet based on Saipan. The Japanese were right to be concerned, for while MacArthur pushed forwards to the Philippines, Nimitz would advance to the northwest towards Japan itself and southwest towards Leyte Gulf. The Mariana Islands had a pivotal role in this strategy for the larger islands of the group – Guam, Saipan and Tinian – offered bases from which B-29s could bomb Japan. More importantly, they also straddled Japan's communications. The Japanese had been feeding reinforcements into the Marianas but many of these troops had fallen prey to the torpedoes of American submarines on route to the Islands. By June 1944 there were some 60,000 Japanese troops garrisoned in the

Marianas, with Saipan the most heavily defended island.

The strength which the United States 5th Fleet brought to the operations in the Marianas was greater than in any previous assault landing. Admiral Mitscher's Fast Carrier Force alone comprised fifteen carriers with over 900 aircraft, seven battleships, twenty-one cruisers, and sixty-nine destroyers. A screen of twenty-eight submarines fanned out ahead of the main fleet and the planes of eleven escort carriers provided close-in cover and ground support. The expeditionary force, under Rear Admiral Richmond Turner, consisted of 127,000 men drawn principally from the 2nd and 4th Marine Divisions and the Army's 27th Infantry Division. The first target was Saipan with attacks against Guam and Tinian planned to follow if satisfactory progress was made with the initial landing operations. Saipan is roughly fourteen miles long by six and a half miles wide, and the landings were planned on a broad front on the west coast near the town of Charan Kanoa. The initial landings would be carried out by the 2nd and 4th Marine Divisions, with the former driving towards the 1,500 foot Mount Tapotchau, while the latter struck out towards the east coast and the airstrip at Aslito. From 11 June, in successive raids over the Marianas, the planes of Admiral Mitscher's fast carriers swept Admiral Nagumo's fighters and bombers from the skies, while the fast battleships of Vice Admiral Willis Lee's squadron, together with the more venerable battleships of the bombardment group, pounded the island defences. On 15 June more than 600 LVT amphibians surged towards the beaches of Saipan carrying some 8,000 marines, and by nightfall, despite heavy casualties, a beach-head five miles long and nearly a mile deep had been established. More than 20,000 marines were now ashore.

Admiral Soemu Toyoda, commanding the Combined Fleet, after the death on active service of Admiral Koga, ordered Vice Admiral Jisaburo Ozawa with the Mobile Fleet of nine carriers, five battleships, and thirteen cruisers to sortie from Tawi Tawi to intercept Mitscher. Warnings from American submarines of Ozawa's approach to the Marianas led Spruance to conclude, incorrectly, that the Mobile Fleet would attack from two directions at once. This delusion influenced Spruance's command decisions throughout the Battle of the Philippine Sea. He cancelled the landing on Guam scheduled for 18 June and ordered Mitscher's task forces to rendezvous 160 miles to the west of Tinian for the task of sinking the Japanese fleet. Neither fleet was entirely certain of the others location, though by dusk on 18 June Ozawa, thanks to the superior range of his search planes, was confident that his bombers would be able to attack the American carriers at dawn. Even so, first blood went to the Americans for early on 19 June the submarine USS *Albacore* torpedoed Ozawa's flagship, the carrier *Taiho*, which as a result of flawed damage control blew up that afternoon. The main carrier action opened with a Japanese strike of 326 aircraft attacking in four waves. Each wave was intercepted by American fighters and torn apart by the anti-aircraft fire of Spruance's battleships. Japanese planes were shot down so rapidly and in such numbers that the engagement was christened the Marianas 'Turkey Shoot'. Only one bomb hit was scored and the Japanese lost 240 aircraft compared to Spruance's twenty-nine. During 19 June the Japanese carrier *Shokaku* was fatally torpedoed by the submarine USS *Cavalla*, and Ozawa turned for Okinawa pursued by the Fast Carrier Force. Mitscher's planes sank the carrier *Hiyo*, and badly damaged the battleship *Haruna* and the carriers *Chiyoda* and *Zuikaku*, though at the

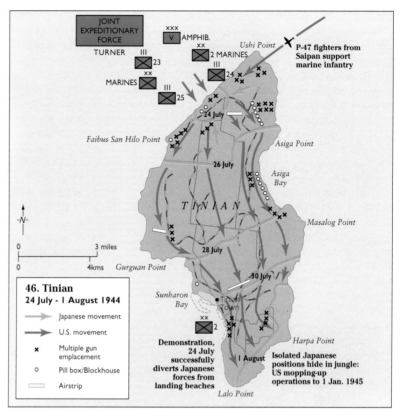

JOINT EXPEDITIONARY FORCE

TURNER

XXX
V AMPHIB.

46. Tinian
24 July - 1 August 1944

Japanese movement

U.S. movement

× Multiple gun emplacement

○ Pill box/Blockhouse

Airstrip

P-47 fighters from Saipan support marine infantry

Ushi Point

Faibus San Hilo Point

Asiga Point

24 July

26 July

Asiga Bay

T I N I A N

Masalog Point

28 July

30 July

Gurguan Point

Sunharon Bay

Tinian Town

Demonstration, 24 July successfully diverts Japanese forces from landing beaches

1 August

Isolated Japanese positions hide in jungle: US mopping-up operations to 1 Jan. 1945

Harpa Point

Lalo Point

0   3 miles
0   4kms

Admiral Nimitz with fellow officers on Saipan: (left to right) Admiral Raymond Spruance, Admiral Ernest King, Admiral Chester Nimitz, and Brigadier General Sanderford Jarman.

cost of ninety-nine aircraft shot down or lost during night recovery.

On Saipan the battle continued to rage and the 27th Division had been landed in support of the marines. The Japanese defenders, however, dissipated their strength in Banzai charges and by 9 July the island had been

47. Strategic View Fall 1944

Japanese movement

U.S. movement

• U.S. submarine deployment

✈ U.S. carrier air strike

KURILE IS.

JAPAN

KOREA

Northern decoy force

FORMOSA

Southern force

BURMA

Pre-invasion air-strikes

SIAM

PHILIPPINE IS.

INDIAN OCEAN

MALAYA   **Centre force**

Singapore   *Brunei*   *Sulu Sea*

U.S. invasion force

DUTCH EAST INDIES
Southern resources area

NEW GUINEA

Banda Sea

AUSTRALIA

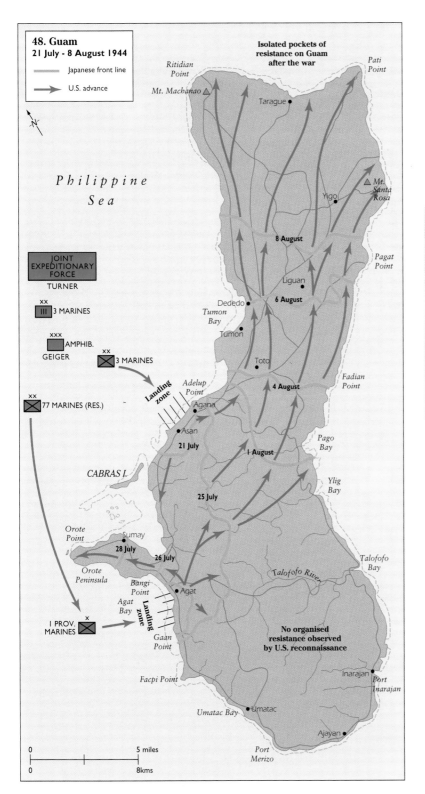

48. Guam
21 July - 8 August 1944

Japanese front line

U.S. advance

N

Philippine Sea

JOINT EXPEDITIONARY FORCE
TURNER

xx
III 3 MARINES

xxx
AMPHIB.
GEIGER

xx
3 MARINES

xx
77 MARINES (RES.)

I PROV.
MARINES x

Ritidian Point

Mt. Machanao △

Taraque ●

Isolated pockets of resistance on Guam after the war

Pati Point

△ *Mt. Santa Rosa*

Yigo ●

8 August

Pagat Point

Liguan ●

6 August

Dededo ●

Tumon Bay

Tumon ●

Toto ●

Fadian Point

Adelup Point

4 August

Agana ●

Landing zone

● Asan

21 July

1 August

Pago Bay

CABRAS I.

25 July

Ylig Bay

Orote Point

Sumay ●

28 July

26 July

Orote Peninsula

Bangi Point

Agat ●

Talofofo River

Talofofo Bay

Agat Bay

Landing zone

Gaan Point

No organised resistance observed by U.S. reconnaissance

Facpi Point

Inarajan ●
Port Inarajan

Umatac Bay ● Umatac

Ajayan ●

0 ——— 5 miles

0 ——— 8kms

Port Merizo

The battleship USS *New Mexico* mounting a shore bombardment to support landings at Guam in July 1944.

The first wave of US Marines land on the beach at Saipan in the Marianas. The marines' hold on the beach became precarious in the face of Japanese counterattacks. The American troops were only able to secure their position when Marine Corps tanks were landed to give close fire support.

secured at a cost of approximately 29,000 Japanese and 16,500 American casualties. Admiral Nagumo, who had led the fleet that attacked Pearl Harbor in December 1941, had committed suicide on 6 July to encourage his troops in their offensive. Guam was systematically bombarded by battle-ships and cruisers for two weeks before the landings carried out by the 3rd Marine Division and the 1st Marine Brigade on 21 July. Most of the visible Japanese defences had been destroyed but those positions hidden in caves survived and the 3rd Marines at Asan and the 1st Brigade at Agat met fierce resistance. Blasting their way from cave to cave, the marines struggled inland where they met and destroyed massed Japanese suicide charges delivered at night. By 8 August the island had been declared secure although sniping continued until the end of the war, and the final Japanese soldier on Guam did not surrender until the 1970s. The 2nd and 4th Marine Divisions landed on the northwest beaches of Tinian on 24 July in the face of intense defensive fire. Supported by P-47's, which dropped napalm for the first time they had crushed the last organised resistance by 1 August. Isolated groups of Japanese held out in caves on the coast and a marine regiment had to be assigned to mopping-up operations.

In the Far East, after the retreat from Burma in the spring of 1942, the British had begun a period of defensive consolidation based on Assam. Effective lines of communication and a well planned logistical system were the key to operations in Burma, and before any major offensive could be contemplated extensive base facilities had to be constructed. It was agreed that India must be capable of maintaining the equivalent of thirty-

A US Marine about to throw a grenade into one of the caves that honeycombed much of the terrain of Saipan. The marines had to resort to grenades, flame throwers and TNT charges to dislodge the Japanese from these rugged hillside positions.

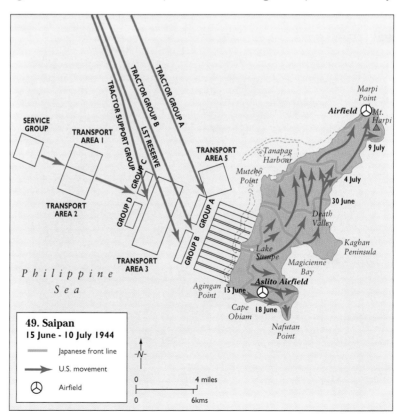

49. Saipan
15 June - 10 July 1944

Japanese front line

U.S. movement

Airfield

-N-

0   4 miles

0   6kms

four divisions, together with eighty-five RAF squadrons and fifteen from the 10th USAAF. The forces based in India would be responsible for the conduct of the campaign in Assam and Burma, the mounting of amphibious operations, the defence of the Northwest Frontier, the training of units in jungle warfare, and the maintenance of internal security across the subcontinent. In a land divided by political and religious conflict, this latter task alone was a massive undertaking requiring the deployment in August 1942, for example, of fifty-seven British and Indian battalions. Much of 1942 and 1943 was spent in developing facilties such as ports, bases, munitions factories, constructing over 220 airfields, and developing a transportation system that could support an army fighting its way into Burma.

The options available to General Sir Archibald Wavell for offensive operations in the dry season starting in November 1942 were limited by factors largely outside his control. A major advance into upper Burma was dependent upon cooperation with Stillwell's Chinese forces and it was clear that they would not be ready to participate in an offensive across the Chindwin and on to Mandalay before November 1943. Moreover, road and rail communications eastwards, and the road to Imphal in particular, needed extending and improving to support any drive into Burma. An amphibious operation against Rangoon, culminating in the capture of this crucial base, could not be undertaken due to a lack of the necessary shipping and landing craft. All that it seemed within Wavell's power to achieve in 1942 was a limited advance on the west coast of Burma in the Arakan. This would essentially be a reconnaissance in force with its main objective the seizure of the Japanese air base on Akyab Island.

LSTs with Coast Guard crews and packed with troops and transports close in on Cape Sansapor.

To prepare the way for the operation in the Arakan the 14th Indian Division, commanded by Major General W Lloyd, pushed forward a brigade to Buthidaung and Maungdaw. There, at the end of October 1942, they encountered the Japanese who were pushing north in an attempt to preempt any move by the British against Akyab. As the British reinforced their drive the Japanese withdrew, enabling the 14th Division to attack towards Akyab along both banks of the River Mayu. In an attempt to reach the mouth of the River on the Mayu Peninsula opposite Akyab, brigade attacks were mounted against both Buthidaung and Donbaik. In assaults against prepared positions the troops of the 14th Division, already on half rations and racked by disease, were as yet no match for the Japanese. After fierce, attritional fighting, with the Japanese as usual exploiting their capacity for flanking attacks though the jungle, the operation was abandoned in March 1943. In April, the Japanese 55th Division struck back with a bold and well executed counteroffensive which drove the British northwards beyond Buthidaung and Maungdaw to their jumping off point in 1942.

Wavell now fell back onto the defensive although with one important and controversial exception. Unable for the moment to meet the Japanese in conventional warfare, he recruited the talents of an exponent of irregular warfare, Major General Orde Wingate. With considerable experience of guerrilla warfare in East Africa, Wingate believed that long range penetration missions could be mounted behind Japanese lines in Burma. Operating independently of other troops, Wingate's brigades, known as Chindits from the *chinthe*, a mythical beast standing guard outside the temples and monasteries of Burma, would carry out attacks on Japanese communications, supply points, and administrative centres. They would be supplied entirely by air, courtesy of the USAAF, and would attempt to distract the

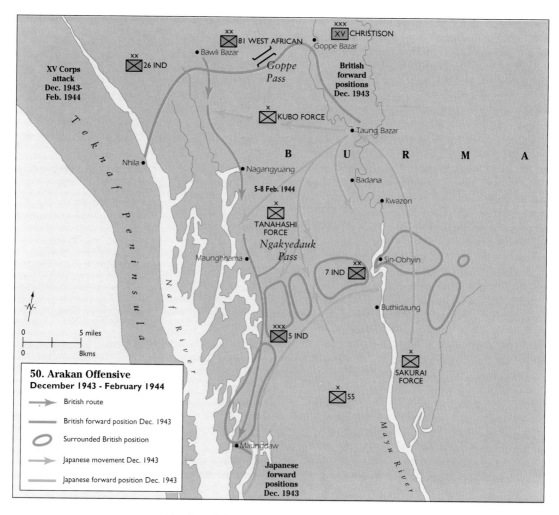

XV Corps attack Dec. 1943-Feb. 1944

British forward positions Dec. 1943

81 WEST AFRICAN

XV CHRISTISON

Goppe Bazar

Bawli Bazar

26 IND

Goppe Pass

KUBO FORCE

Taung Bazar

B U R M A

Nhila

Nagangyuang

Badana

5-8 Feb. 1944

Kwazon

TANAHASHI FORCE

Ngakyedauk Pass

Maunghnama

7 IND

Sin-Obhyin

Buthidaung

5 IND

SAKURAI FORCE

55

Maungdaw

Japanese forward positions Dec. 1943

Teknaf Peninsula

Naf River

Mayu River

50. Arakan Offensive
December 1943 - February 1944

→ British route

— British forward position Dec. 1943

⬭ Surrounded British position

→ Japanese movement Dec. 1943

— Japanese forward position Dec. 1943

0   5 miles

0   8kms

attention of Japanese units facing the Chinese in Yunnan. The first Chindit expedition, 3,000 strong, comprised one British battalion, one Gurkha battalion, a commando company, and a mule transport company, together with a battalion of Burma Rifles. On 13 and 14 February 1943, the Chindits crossed the Chindwin and marched into Burma. They did not inflict great damage on the Japanese war effort, but they demonstrated to the enemy that a defensive perimeter in the jungle could not be counted secure, and their endeavours provided a significant boost to morale in India and Great Britain. In all they marched over 1,000 miles through enemy territory and learned many lessons concerning jungle warfare, air supply, and communications. The cost was high: 800 of the Chindits died on the mission and many of those who returned were unfit for further combat.

In June 1943 General Sir Claude Auchinleck succeeded Wavell as Commander-in-Chief in India, and found his options for offensive action almost as restricted as those of his predecessor. For much of the next year, he was able to plan, but not execute, strategic operations, and most of what he intended to achieve was dependent upon American support. British operations in Burma would rely to a very real extent upon supply by

American transport aircraft, and any major offensive would have to be linked to the southwards advance from Ledo of American-led Chinese forces, and to the westward movement of Chinese troops from Yunnan. These problems were removed from Auchinleck's domain with the creation of a new inter-Allied command in the Far East. Known as South East Asia Command (SEAC), its Supreme Commander would assume control of all Allied operations – land, sea and air — in the Indian Ocean, the Bay of Bengal and adjacent territories. Vice-Admiral Lord Louis Mountbatten assumed the office of Supreme Commander in October 1943, with Lieutenant General Stilwell as his deputy. On land, in addition to the Chinese and American forces in the theatre, Mountbatten could call upon the 14th Army (IV Corps and XV Corps) commanded by Lieutenant General 'Bill' Slim. As one of the outstanding generals of World War II, Slim made a signal contribution to the Allied campaign in Burma and to the 14th Army. Commanding nearly one million men — Indian, British, Gurkha, Burmese, East and West Africans, Kachin and Karen – Slim was an astute tactician who knew the strengths and weaknesses of both his own troops and those of the enemy. He was to take the 'Forgotten' 14th Army from the defensive to a victory of stunning proportions.

In January 1944 Mountbatten initiated a limited advance by 14th Army with IV Corps tackling the Japanese west of the Chindwin, XV Corps pushing towards Buthidaung and Maungdaw, and a second, larger Chindit operation, involving some 9,000 troops, deployed to form offensive strongholds behind enemy lines. As the British attack unfolded, it became apparent that the Japanese facing IV Corps (Lieutenant General G Scoones) on the Imphal front and XV Corps (Lieutenant General Philip Christison) in the Arakan, were in much greater strength than anticipated. Both the British and the Japanese were in fact in the process of launching offensive operations over the same ground, and at virtually the same time. As Christison's 7th Division advanced in February, it encountered the Japanese 55th Division advancing to undertake its own Arakan offensive (Operation HA-GO).

Although the western defensive perimeter of the Greater East Asia Co-Prosperity Sphere had been fixed as the border between Burma and India, the easy successes of their opening campaign led the Japanese Southern Army to consider an offensive against northeast Assam. The 15th Army planned to deploy units from the 18th, 33rd and 55th Divisions, in an advance to Imphal, Kohima, Dimapur, Silchar, Golaghat, and Ledo, but the reverses suffered by the their forces in the South Pacific caused Imperial General Headquarters to freeze the operation. The Japanese strategy in Burma for most of 1942–43 was therefore based on defensive measures only. By the beginning of 1944, however, with the absolute defence line under ever greater pressure in the Pacific, the prospect of a British offensive in northern Burma was of great concern to the Japanese since it threatened French Indochina and Siam, the weakest links in their defence perimeter. The first operation by the Chindits, although inflicting negligible damage, had caused doubts among the Japanese command as to their ability to hold a defensive line positioned in Burma. The 1942 plan, straightforward in conception but dangerous in execution, was reinstated by the new commander of the 15th Army, Lieutenant General Renya Mutaguchi. Its aim was to secure Burma through forestalling a British advance by taking Imphal, and then, having seized Kohima, to sever the line of communication in north Assam to China and destroy the airfields ferrying supplies to the Chinese and American forces. This would, the Japanese hoped, paralyse any Allied offensive drive across the India-Burma border. The role of the preliminary Arakan operation (HA-GO), by the 55th Division of the Japanese 28th Army, was to force Slim to commit his reserves in defence of the important port of Chittagong and its airfield. The 15th Army, deploying the 15th, 31st, and 33rd Divisions, would then find its advance to Imphal and Kohima (U-GO) considerably eased.

At first in the Arakan all went well for the Japanese and the 55th Division succeeded in encircling the 7th Indian Division. Refusing to allow this tactical reverse to degenerate into blind retreat, Slim ordered the Division to hold fast, promising them resupply by air while reinforcements fought their way through. In what became known as the Battle of the 'Admin Box', the 7th Division held fast at Sinzweya until the 5th, 26th, and 36th Divisions reached them. The Japanese were not only defeated on the ground in the Arakan for during these operations they also lost control of the air. The arrival of additional Spitfire fighters in India helped the Royal Air Force to achieve a general superiority over the Burma front. This meant that Allied air transports could now deliver their loads almost without opposition, even in Japanese air space. This was a vital victory in the reconquest of Burma.

Undeterred by these setbacks the Japanese launched their main offensive on 15 March 1944. Slim had previously decided that when this happened IV Corps would withdraw its forward divisions – 17th and 20th – to the Imphal plain, thus setting a trap for the Japanese in an area where the 14th Army would be close to its base, and where its superiority in armour could be exploited to the full. The forward troops fell back before the Japanese, not without some alarms, and IV Corps formed a defensive ring round Imphal. In the meantime, eighty miles to the north, the garrison of Kohima was attacked at the end of the first week in April. The 161st Brigade, which had not been moved to Imphal with the remainder of the 5th Division, was still at Kimapur, and it managed to slip one battalion into the Kohima perimeter on the day after the Japanese attack began. The Brigade's other two battalions deployed to the north, but within sight of Kohima, and across the road to Dimpaur, where the 2nd (British) Division was already preparing a counterattack. For twelve bloody but crucial days, the garrison of Kohima held out in appalling conditions against the concentrated might of the Japanese 31st Division. The brigades of the 2nd Division went straight into action as they moved forward, and by 15 April they had linked up with the 161st Brigade outside Kohima. This enabled the latter, three days later, to advance and break the siege. Even so the Battle of Kohima was to last another six weeks, with the heaviest fighting falling on the 2nd and 7th Divisions, until on 3 June the Japanese abandoned the struggle and began to retreat back into Burma.

The contest for Imphal continued until 22 June, when the 2nd Division, pushing quickly south, linked up with the 5th Indian Division twenty-five miles north of Imphal. Lieutenant General Geoffrey Scoones (IV Corps) and Lieutenant General Montagu Stopford (XXXIII Corps) now consolidated their victory by seizing Ukhrul, and by blocking the escape routes between there and the Chindwin for the retreating, and now starving, Japanese 15th and 31st Divisions. From its original strength of 85,000 men the 15th Army suffered 53,000 casualties and the battles for the Arakan, Imphal and Kohima proved to be SEAC's decisive campaign in the Far East. At vital stages in the battle, the Chinese divisions of Stilwell's Northern Combat Area Com-

General Sir Archibald Wavell, Supreme Commander of the ABDA area in 1942 and subsequently Commander-in-Chief India, greets officers and men of the 20th Indian Division.

mand, supported by an American commando force (5307th Provisional Regiment) known after its commander, Brigadier General Frank Merrill, as 'Merrill's Maurauders', were able to exert pressure on the Japanese along the Salween to assist the 14th Army. Reconquest of Burma was now possible.

SEAC planned two major operations based on 14th Army's success: Operation CAPITAL for the land invasion of Burma, and Operation DRACULA for the capture of Rangoon by amphibious assault. By late November 1944, 14th Army had launched its campaign for the reconquest of Burma with XXXIII Corps, supported by the 11th East African Division, fighting on through the monsoon to push the Japanese across the Chindwin and back against the Irrawaddy. Initially, Slim expected to have to fight a decisive battle before he reached the Irrawaddy, probably around Shwebo, but as IV Corps pressed on it became clear that the Japanese were deliberately yielding ground and falling back across the river. Accordingly, while the 19th Indian Division continued to drive for Mandalay as though nothing had changed, Slim secretly transferred the majority of IV Corps one hundred miles to the west and then despatched the 7th Indian Division, covered by a screen of East African troops and observing strict radio silence, up the Kale valley to gain a bridgehead across the Irrawaddy at Nyaungu near

Supply trucks moving up the tortuous route to Tamu, a link in the lines of communication developed to maintain the 14th Army in Burma.

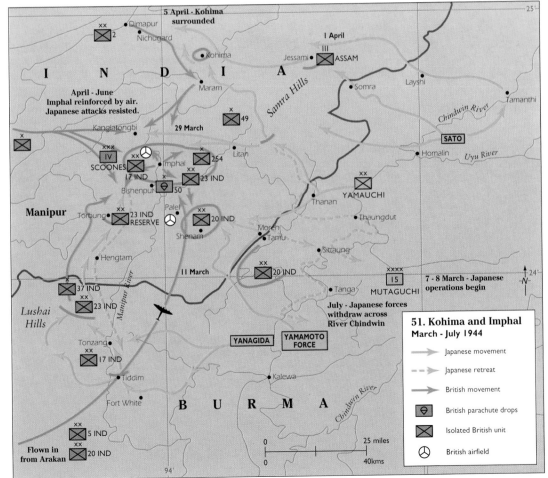

51. Kohima and Imphal
March - July 1944

Pakkoku. The crossing would outflank the Japanese defences to the south, and would place IV Corps within striking distance of the vital Japanese supply and communication centre of Meiktila.

While the 19th Division and XXXIII Corps fixed the enemy's attention and fought their way across the Irrawaddy on 12 February 1945, IV Corps also crossed the river but against comparatively light opposition. At a stroke, the Japanese 15th and 33rd Armies were all but cut off from their bases in South Burma and their communications with the 28th Army in Arakan severed. By 3 March Stopford's armoured spearhead had captured Meiktila and in a ferocious battle, during which it was supplied by air, IV Corps defeated counterattacks by two Japanese divisions and held on to the vital communications centre. To the northeast XXXIII Corps had taken Mandalay

Major General Orde Wingate visiting a Chindit column in the jungle in Burma.

Soldiers of the 10th Gurkha Rifles clearing Japanese positions on 'Scraggy', one of the hills in the Shenam Saddle range on the road to Imphal, in Burma, which witnessed bitter fighting in April 1944.

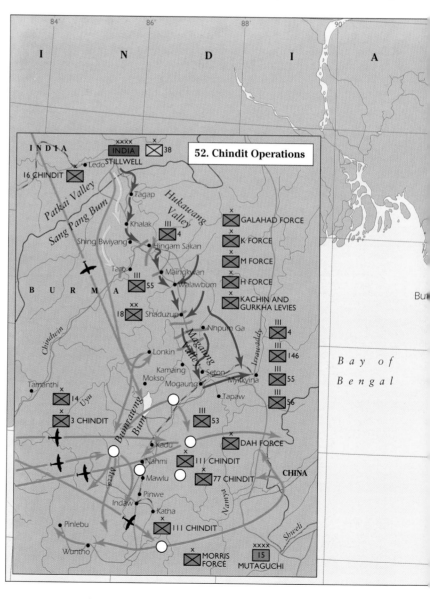

52. Chindit Operations

after some bitter street fighting and by the end of March had linked up with IV Corps. Caught between XXXIII and IV Corps the Japanese 15th and 33rd Armies began to disintegrate and by April 1945 they were all but finished as a fighting force. Pushing south down the Irrawaddy valley, the leading troops of 14th Army had reached Pegu, only fifty miles from Rangoon, when their advance was halted by the Monsoon. As a result operation DRACULA was activated and Rangoon fell to an amphibious assault by the 26th Division, supported by the 50th Parachute Brigade airborne landings.

That DRACULA had been possible was due to the operations carried out by XV Corps in the Arakan. Christison's troops had fought against fierce Japanese resistance on the Mayu Peninsula and in the Kaladan Valley, and had also taken Akyab and Ramree Islands from where air cover could be

Lieutenant-General Sir William Slim, General Officer Commanding-in-Chief, 14th Army, masterminded the victory of the British forces in Burma.

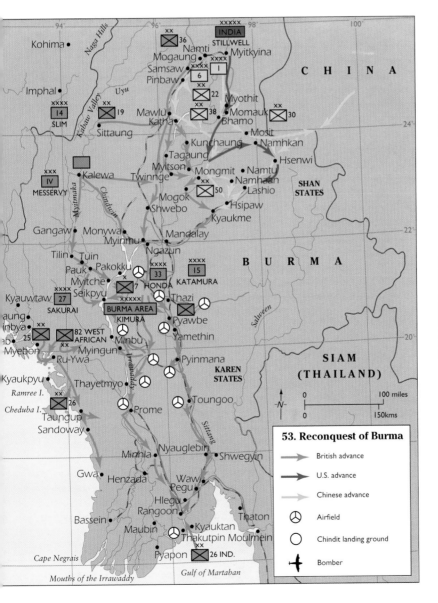

Lieutenant General Joseph Stilwell (sitting to the left of the driver in the first jeep), holding a carbine, leads a team of American staff officers to visit advance troops of the Chinese forces in Burma in 1944.

53. Reconquest of Burma

→ British advance
→ U.S. advance
→ Chinese advance
⊗ Airfield
○ Chindit landing ground
✚ Bomber

The Supreme Allied Commander South East Asia, Admiral Lord Louis Mountbatten, meeting soldiers of the Kenya Battalion, The King's African Rifles after fighting in the Kabaw Valley, Burma. Troops from West and East Africa formed almost as large an element in the army in Burma as those from Great Britain. These soldiers gained a reputation as brave and ferocious fighters.

A Sherman tank in Burma advancing with infantry in the push towards Mandalay. The most effective use of armour in a jungle context in the Pacific War was made by the British and Indian Armies in Burma.

mounted for the operations against Rangoon. The surviving units of the Japanese 15th and 33rd Armies, which had retreated into the mountains east of the Sittang, now attempted to open an escape route for the 28th Army trapped in the Pegu Yomas. From June to August 1945, in the swamps, paddy fields and deluging rain of the Sittang Valley, the 14th Army fought to eliminate the majority of the 16,000 Japanese troops who were attempting to reach Siam and Malaya. In a little over three years the Japanese victory in Burma had been completely overturned, and only the Japanese surrender prevented the amphibious assault on Malaya (Operation ZIPPER) being carried out.

While Nimitz was pressing forward in the central Pacific, the US 7th Fleet, together with the VII Amphibious Force, landed troops from the 24th and 41st Infantry Divisions at Hollandia in New Guinea on 22 April 1944. The Japanese garrison in the area retreated to the hills, leaving the air strips in Allied control. Leiutenant General Eichelberger next took Noemfor and Biak Islands before pressing on to Morotai and Peleliu midway between New Guinea and the Philippines. On 15 September 1944, the 1st Marine Division landed on Peleliu while army troops assaulted Morotai. To avoid the pre-landing bombardment, the Japanese had established their main defensive positions inland and the marines came inshore without incident. As they sought to establish themselves, however, they were hit by mortar and machine gun fire and later attacked by tanks and by Japanese troops in suicide charges.

Official presidential approval launched MacArthur's invasion of the Philippines at a time when opposition to its execution was considerable, particularly from the highest echelons of the navy. This was essentially a personal triumph for MacArthur, but it was to involve his troops in some of the hardest fighting of the Pacific War. The Philippines comprise approximately 7,000 islands only four of which were of overriding military importance: Mindanao in the south of the Archipelago, Leyte and Mindoro in the centre and Luzon in the north. Although MacArthur was directed by the Joint Chiefs to occupy Mindanao and Leyte, it had not yet been decided whether his next assault would be upon Luzon or Formosa. With Pacific Fleet submarines taking an ever increasing toll of Japanese shipping, the supply of raw material to the home islands was falling steadily. The seizure of either Formosa or the Philippines would eliminate these supplies altogether.

For the first amphibious assault against Leyte, MacArthur deployed a Northern Attack Force (Rear Admiral Daniel Barbey) and a Southern Attack Force (Vice Admiral Theodore Wilkinson) totalling over 200,000 men of the 6th Army and 500 ships. The landings were to be mounted by Kinkaid's 7th Fleet which would have the support of eighteen of the 3rd Fleet's escort carriers together with Admiral Jesse Oldendorf's battleship Bombardment Force. Halsey's Fast Carrier Force would supply distant support to the landings, and would also seek to intercept any sweep by ships of the Combined Fleet. The enemy was indeed planning a fleet action for they realised that the American amphibious forces would be operating with only carrier air support. The Japanese would have the advantage of land based air support and they intended to sortie with the Combined Fleet under its protection. The Japanese plan for the defence of the Philippines, SHO-1, recognised that only a portion of the Archipelago could be garrisoned and allocated priority to Luzon. On land the defence of the Philippines rested with 14th Area Army, commanded by Lieutenant General Tomoyuki Yamashita, and the 4th

Air Army. There were some ten infantry divisions and one armoured division available to Yamashita. Leyte is just over 100 miles in length and between fifteen and forty five miles wide, with terrain that is mostly mountainous and inhospitable except for level areas in the northeast and west. Mac-Arthur's initial objectives were the airfields at Dulag and Tacloban, and on 20 October, 1944 the US XXIV Corps (7th and 96th Army Divisions) landed near the former, and X Corps (1st Cavalry and 24th Division) three miles south of the latter.

The Japanese plan for a fleet action once again involved complex maneouvres and the use of a decoy; on this occasion Admiral Ozawa's Northern Force comprising six carriers of varying tonnage and design. Ozawa's role was to tempt Halsey away from Leyte Gulf, thereby exposing the invasion fleet to attack from the north by Admiral Kurita's Central Force, and from the south by Vice Admiral Nishimura's Southern Force. Kurita sailed with five battleships, including the super battleships *Musashi* and *Yamato*, and twelve cruisers, while Nishimura's main strength lay in two battleships and one heavy cruiser. Halsey was hit first on 24 October, losing the light carrier *Princeton* to a bombing attack, but that day his planes found both the Central and Southern Forces. He ordered his carriers to concentrate their attacks on the Central Force and after losing the giant battleship *Musashi*, Kurita turned away westwards towards the Sibuyan Sea. Admiral Oldendorf's Bombardment Group of battleships and cruisers was sent south to guard the Surigao Strait and during the night of 24–25 October, it intercepted Nishimura's Southern Force. After running the gauntlet of repeated torpedo attacks by American PT boats, the Japanese ran foul of five destroyers which also launched torpedoes. The battleship *Fuso* was hit and forced to pull out of line, while three Japanese destroyers were sunk. Nishimura next encountered the radar controlled fire of Oldendorf's six battleships, and despite the fact that five of them had been damaged at Pearl Harbor, their guns proved too much for the Japanese. The battleship *Yamashiro* was wrecked and the heavy cruiser *Mogami* badly damaged. At this point the rear cruiser-destroyer squadron of the Southern Force, under Vice Admiral Kiyohide Shima, blundered on to the scene, and Shima's flagship, the cruiser *Nachi*, collided with the crippled *Mogami*. The Southern Force was finished and Shima reversed course with his remaining ships. Oldendorf's casualties amounted to a single destroyer damaged as it was caught in the crossfire between the two fleets.

Far to the north of the Surigao Strait, Halsey and the 3rd Fleet were preparing to deal with Ozawa's carriers off Cape Engano. Halsey planned to take his three carrier task groups in pursuit of Ozawa and at the same time to form a fourth group, Task Force 34, composed of four battleships and five cruisers under Vice Admiral Willis Lee. From Halsey's signals it appeared to Kinkaid with the 7th Fleet, to Admiral Nimitz in Hawaii, and to Admiral King in Washington that he had left Task Force 34 behind to guard the San Bernardino Strait and the transports anchored in Leyte Gulf. Halsey, however, had taken Lee's battleships north in pursuit of Ozawa and Task Force 34 had not yet been formed. Meanwhile Kurita and the Central Force, belaboured into turning back towards the San Bernardino Strait by the Combined Fleet, bore down on Admiral Clifton Sprague's six escort carriers off Samar shortly before 7.00 am on 25 October. In a vain attempt to outrun Kurita's battleships and cruisers, Sprague steamed south, making smoke while his ground attack aircraft and destroyer escorts fought a

Aerial shot of the Japanese battleship *Yamashiro* under attack by US Navy planes at the Battle of Leyte Gulf in October 1944.

desperate rearguard action.

The Japanese, now in hot pursuit, were alarmed to find torpedo tracks lancing towards them while a circus of aircraft swarmed about their masts. The battleship *Yamato* turned away to the north and fell behind the running fight, but the rest of Kurita's force closed rapidly on the American carriers. The escort carrier *Gambier* and a number of destroyers were sunk by gunfire, but Sprague's surviving ships were saved by the intervention of torpedo bombers from Admiral Stump's group of escort carriers, and by Kurita's order that his ships should break off the action to come to the protection of the now isolated *Yamato*. Once again at the very moment of victory a Japanese commander had turned his fleet because of the fear of losing ships. Horrified by Sprague's desperate calls for help, Nimitz sent a signal to Halsey which, after padding had been added to confuse Japanese cryptographers, read:

'Where is, repeat, where is, Task Force 34? The world wonders.'

Halsey was furious at this apparent insult and it was only after a studied tardiness that he sent the Task Force and a carrier group south to assist the 7th Fleet. During its pursuit to the north the planes of the 3rd Fleet had accounted for all four of Ozawa'a carriers and the Battle of Leyte Gulf ended as a resounding American victory. There was a disturbing coda to the battle when, in the first example of what was to become a regular tactic of the closing stages of the war in the Pacific, Japanese suicide planes targetted the carriers of the 3rd Fleet. As Japanese air power fell further and

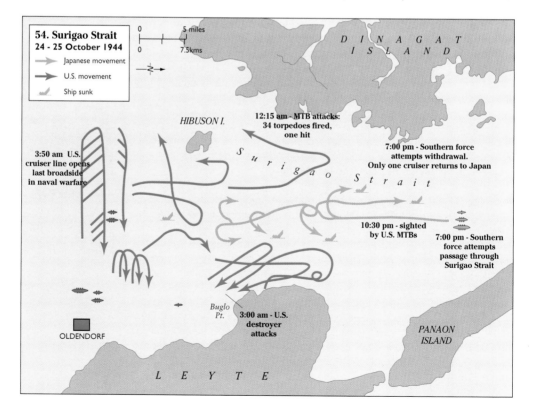

54. Surigao Strait
24 - 25 October 1944

0 — 5 miles
0 — 7.5kms

→ Japanese movement
➤ U.S. movement
⚓ Ship sunk

DINAGAT ISLAND

HIBUSON I.

12:15 am - MTB attacks: 34 torpedoes fired, one hit

7:00 pm - Southern force attempts withdrawal. Only one cruiser returns to Japan

3:50 am U.S. cruiser line opens last broadside in naval warfare

Surigao Strait

10:30 pm - sighted by U.S. MTBs

7:00 pm - Southern force attempts passage through Surigao Strait

OLDENDORF

Buglo Pt.

3:00 am - U.S. destroyer attacks

PANAON ISLAND

L E Y T E

further behind that of the United States, Admiral Takijiro Ohnishi, commanding the 1st Air Fleet, conceived the tactic of deliberately crashing aircraft into warships in order to guarantee a direct hit. Special air attack units, which were popularly known as Kamikaze from the Japanese for 'Divine Wind', were formed and sent into action against Sprague's carriers off Leyte. Admiral Ohnishi had realised that the Kamikaze could only be a short term weapon, but Imperial General Headquarters was so carried away by their early successes that it issued a general order that all Japan's armed forces should adopt the suicide attack. Altogether, nearly 2,500 Kamikaze pilots were to die for the emperor during World War II.

The Japanese had originally planned to fight the decisive battle for the Philippines on Luzon where there was sufficient area for a defence in depth, and where their supply system was at its most effective. On 18 October, however, as a result of widely exaggerated claims of the damage inflicted by Japanese aircraft on Halsey's 3rd Fleet at the 'Victory of Taiwan', Imperial General Headquarters issued orders that Leyte would be defended to the utmost and its garrison reinforced. By early December Japanese fighting strength on Leyte had risen to 65,000 men. As a result the US 6th Army discovered that it had a bitter fight on its hands when it encountered the Japanese 1st Infantry Division on 'Breakneck Ridge'. Superbly positioned in skilfully camouflaged tunnels, caves and trenches, the 1st Division maintained their hold on the rugged peaks despite determined American attacks. Only after the US 77th Division had made an amphibious landing near Deposito, and fought their way into the Japanese supply and reinforcement base at Ormoc, did enemy resistance begin to

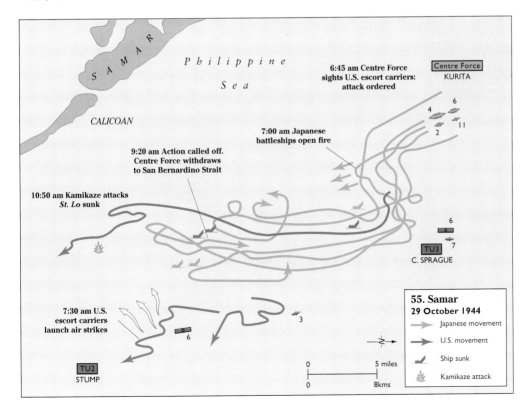

SAMAR

CALICOAN

Philippine Sea

6:45 am Centre Force sights U.S. escort carriers: attack ordered

Centre Force
KURITA

7:00 am Japanese battleships open fire

9:20 am Action called off. Centre Force withdraws to San Bernardino Strait

10:50 am Kamikaze attacks
St. Lo sunk

4
6
2
11

6

TU3 7
C. SPRAGUE

7:30 am U.S. escort carriers launch air strikes

3

6

TU2
STUMP

55. Samar
29 October 1944

→ Japanese movement
→ U.S. movement
⚓ Ship sunk
✹ Kamikaze attack

0   5 miles
0   8kms

falter. Although their was more fighting ahead the Japanese garrison was now split into pockets and cut off from support from Luzon.

The unexpected length of the fighting on Leyte and the delays in the completion of airstrips led to the postponement of the assaults on Mindaro and Luzon. It was not until 15 December that an army brigade landed near San Jose on Mindoro to deal with the 500 strong Japanese garrison, but before the end of the month two airfields had been constructed and planes were operating against Japanese positions on Luzon. There were approximately 250,000 poorly equipped Japanese troops on Luzon deployed in three defensive formations: the Shimbu Group (80,000 men), the Kembu Group (30,000 men) and the Shobu Group (140,000 men). The strongest, the Shobu Group, was responsible for the defence of Lingayen Gulf where the Japanese themselves had landed in December, 1941. MacArthur's planned assault on Luzon called for an amphibious landing at the southern end of the Gulf, followed by the construction of airfields, exploitation into the Central Plain and the seizure of Manila. This operation would be the responsibility of the 6th Army, under General Krueger, together with the 7th Fleet under Admiral Kinkaid. Admiral Halsey with the 3rd Fleet, supported by B-29s from China and aircraft from Leyte and Mindoro, would provide air cover and target Japanese bases on Luzon and Formosa. As the amphibious force steamed for Lingayen Gulf on 2 January 1945 these air defence measures appeared less than effective. The invasion convoy was forced to run a gaunlet of Kamikaze attacks which sank or damaged thirty ships.

Japanese ground forces did not seriously contest the landing by I and XIV Corps at Lingayen Gulf on 9 January 1945, since General Yamashita had realised that after the losses on Leyte he could not hope to defend the whole of Luzon. Accordingly he issued orders for a gradual withdrawal into three mountain strongholds located around Baguio, in the Cabusilian Mountains, and in the mountains to the east of Manila. To forestall any attempt Yamashita might make to fight a protracted battle for the Bataan Peninsula, troops of the US XI Corps (38th Division and 34th Regimental Combat Team) landed in Subic Bay and near San Antonio. By 5 February

General Douglas MacArthur wading ashore with a group of American and Philippine Army officers at Leyte Island during the invasion of the Philippines.

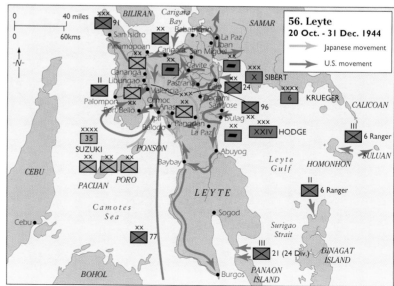

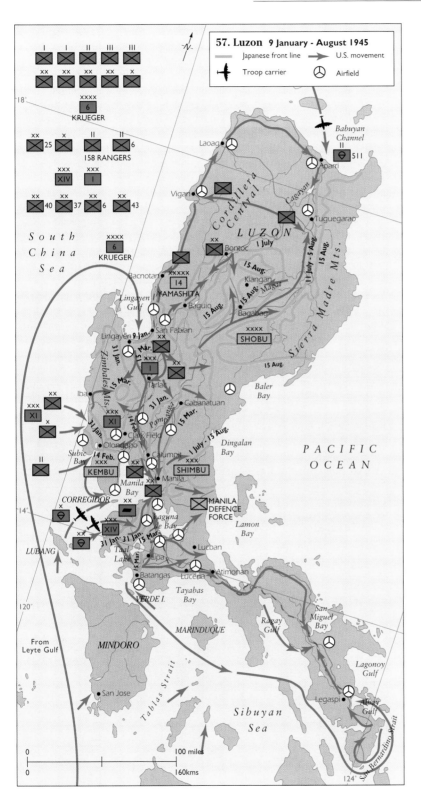

57. Luzon 9 January - August 1945

Japanese front line ——— U.S. movement ➜

Troop carrier ✈ Airfield ⊘

South China Sea

PACIFIC OCEAN

KRUEGER

158 RANGERS

XIV   I

KRUEGER

YAMASHITA

SHOBU

KEMBU

SHIMBU

MANILA DEFENCE FORCE

CORREGIDOR

LUBANG

From Leyte Gulf

MINDORO

MARINDUQUE

Sibuyan Sea

General Yamashita, the 'Tiger of Malaya', surrenders the Japanese Army in the Philippines to Generals Wainright and Percival, both defeated previously by Yamashita at Corregidor and Singapore respectively.

they had linked up with XIV Corps at San Fernando. Clark Field had been captured by XIV Corps on 1 February and rapid progress had been made towards Manila by the 1st Cavalry Division and the 37th Division, and by the 11th Airborne Division advancing on the city from the direction of Tagaytay. On 4 February the northern portion of the city was occupied, but although Yamashita had declared Manila an open city, Rear Admiral Iwabachi, using 16,000 naval personnel, continued to fight from street to street in its defence. The battle for Manila reduced the city to rubble and the last Japanese resistance did not end until 4 March. The island of Corregidor fell to a combined airborne and amphibious assault after its defenders were hunted through its complex of caves and tunnels. Everywhere the Japanese were gradually forced back and by 15 March they were largely contained in three isolated pockets, much as Yamashita had predicted. Thereafter the American troops fought against dogged resistance in their efforts to eliminate these pockets, and Yamashita still had 50,000 men under arms when he finally surrendered on 15 August 1945. It has been estimated that almost 200,000 Japanese died during the battle for the Philippines, while US ground forces suffered over 44,000 casualties.

While the fighting in the Philippines continued, the strategic emphasis shifted northwards with the assault on Iwo Jima. Measuring little more than eight square miles in extent, Iwo Jima is a plateau of volcanic ash dominated from its southern end by the 556 foot Mount Suribachi, an extinct volcano. Although the island was distinctly unattractive as real estate it was supremely important as a strategic staging post on the route to Japan. Situated roughly half way between Tokyo and Saipan, Iwo Jima already possessed two operational airfields while a third was under construction. These fields were only 660 miles, or three hours flying time, from Tokyo as opposed to the 2,800 miles of the round trip from the Marianas. Moreover, B-29s based on Iwo Jima could be escorted all the way to their targets by both P-51 Mustangs and P-47 Thunderbolts. The Japanese defenders of the island numbered approximately 21,000 men commanded by Lieu-

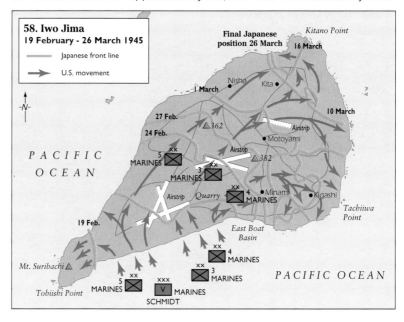

58. Iwo Jima
19 February - 26 March 1945

tenant-General Tadamichi Kuribayashi, and they had prepared a formidable defence in depth. Kuribayashi had decided upon a static defence anchored on Mount Suribachi, and he did not intend to contest the initial landings on the beaches. Instead, Suribachi and the plateau between Airfields 2 and 3 were heavily fortified with over 600 gun emplacements and pillboxes, as well as a complex system of cave defences and deep shelters. It was clear from previous experience that the garrison of Iwo Jima would fight with tenacity and purpose to the death.

In view of Japanese strength on the island and the limited room for manoeuvre during the assault and exploitation phases, it was clear to Nimitz that the conquest of Iwo Jima would require a toe-to-toe fire fight with the defenders. An extended aerial bombardment of the island was therefore carried out by the 7th USAAF from the Marianas, and this was followed by three days of naval gunfire bombardment. Admiral Spruance with the 5th Fleet was in overall command of the American operation while the actual task of capturing Iwo Jima was given to the 5th US Amphibious Corps, comprising the 3rd, 4th, and 5th Marine Divisions. During preliminary reconnaissance and mine clearance by American frogmen and engineers the Japanese opened fire, thereby revealing many of their gun positions. As a result, when the bombardment group closed to within 2,500 yards of the shore immediately prior to the landings they were able to eliminate a good many defence positions. Even so the 4th and 5th Divisions, when they came ashore, found themselves pinned down by exceptionally accurate fire which was being directed by observers on Suribachi. Nevertheless before the end of the day the marines had cut the island in two, and after some of the most bitter fighting in the Pacific the 3rd Marines scaled Suribachi on 23 February. Thereafter, the remains of the Japanese garrison, trapped in the northern portion of the island, expended much of their strength in suicide charges and Iwo Jima was declared secure on 26 March. Its capture had cost nearly 25,000 American casualties, but already on 4 March a B-29 returning from a raid on Japan had

From their exposed position on the landing beach, US Marines fire a 37mm gun at the network of Japanese foritifications on Mount Suribachi, following the United States invasion of Iwo Jima in February 1945.

made an emergency landing on the island. By the end of the war over 2,000 B-29s had made successful emergency landings on Iwo Jima, and the 24,000 crew members they carried thereby escaped death or injury.

Once the possibility of an invasion of Formosa had been finally rejected, orders for the assault upon Okinawa in the Ryukyu Islands were issued. The strategic value of Okinawa lay in its position only 350 miles from Kyushu, the southernmost island of Japan, and in its suitability for airfield construction and fleet anchorages. To gain these prizes Nimitz had to wrest the island from the 100,000 men of the Japanese 32nd Army in the face of mass Kamikaze attacks and possible sorties by the surviving warships of the Combined Fleet. Nimitz assembled a mighty armada which in itself constituted a logistical nightmare. Some 290,000 Allied troops and 1,500 ships would descend on Okinawa from 1 April 1945. The landings were to be carried out by the four army and three marine divisions of the 10th Army, under the command of Lieutenant General Simon Bolivar Buckner. Although it meant the sacrifice of any element of surprise, Nimitz decided to isolate Okinawa through air strikes against Formosa, Hong Kong, and Japan, an operation which claimed over 500 enemy aircraft. On 26 March preliminary landings were carried out to put troops ashore on the Kerama Retto group, twenty miles south of Okinawa, and artillery on Keise Shima. An eight day bombardment of Okinawa was carried out by battleships and heavy cruisers. While the battle for Okinawa raged, the 5th Fleet was diverted from the task of dealing with Kamikaze attacks to meet a suicide sortie by the superbattleship *Yamato*. With only enough fuel for the outward voyage, Vice Admiral Seiichi Ito sailed with the *Yamato*, the cruiser *Yahagi* and eight destroyers to attack American shipping off Okinawa. Mitscher deployed three task groups and some 380 aircraft from Task Force 58 against Ito, and by the afternoon of 7 April the *Yamato* had been sunk by multiple torpedo and bomb hits and by internal explosions. Throughout the Okinawa operation the British Pacific Fleet acted as the left flank guard for the expeditionary force. It was designated as Task Force 57 and comprised the battleships *Howe* and *King George V*, the four fleet carriers *Indefatigable*, *Indomitable*, *Illustrious*, and *Victorious*, and cruisers and destroyers.

Key to movements

1. 17 October - U.S. landings

2. Centre force sails from Brunei

3. 23 October - 2 U.S. submarines sink 2 heavy cruisers

4. TF 38 arrives off Philippines

5. Southern force enters Mindinao Sea

6. 24 October - up to 7:40 pm U.S. carriers launch air strikes on Japanese Centre force

7. Southern force engaged by U.S. force

8. Southern force withdraws

9. 24 October 4:40 pm - Northern decoy force detected by U.S. patrol aircraft

10. Halsey orders all TG's north of Cape Engano to engage Japanese Northern force

11. Japanese Centre force passes through Strait undetected

12. Centre force detects U.S. escort carrier force near Samar Island, general attack ordered

13. U.S. forces engage Northern decoy force

14. Halsey orders Task Groups 38.1 and 38.2 south to aid escort carrier force under attack by Japanese Centre force

15. Japanese Centre force breaks off action, withdraws through San Bernadino Strait

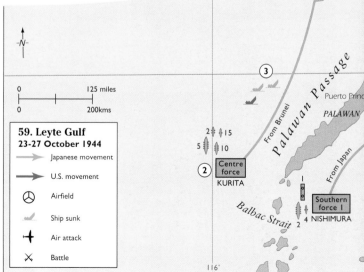

59. Leyte Gulf
23-27 October 1944

→ Japanese movement

➔ U.S. movement

⊗ Airfield

⤸ Ship sunk

✛ Air attack

✕ Battle

0 — 125 miles

0 — 200kms

-N-

116°

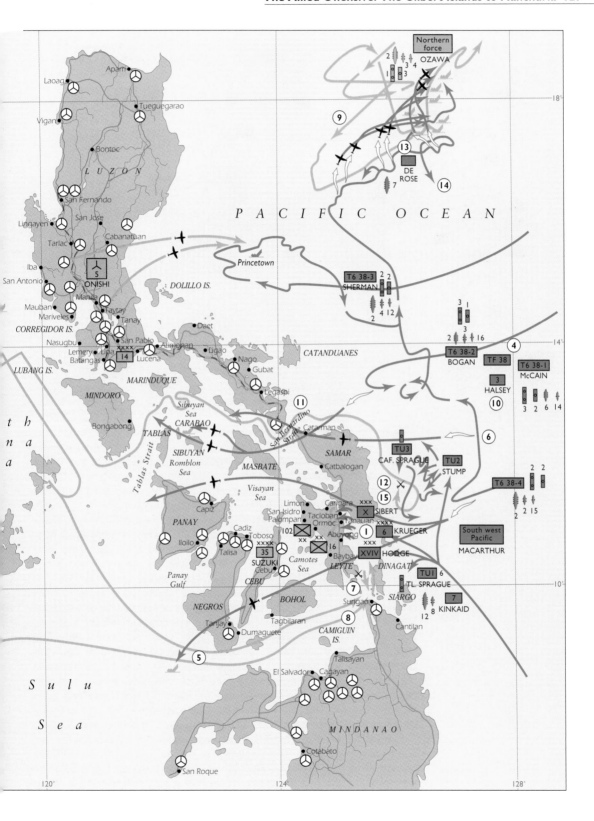

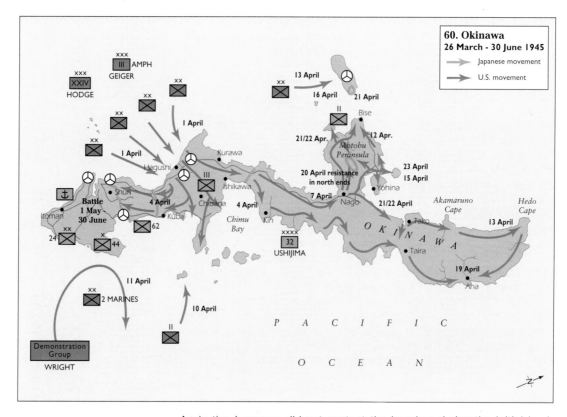

60. Okinawa
26 March - 30 June 1945

Japanese movement
U.S. movement

Again the Japanese did not contest the beaches during the initial landings on Okinawa, but as a precaution, while the real landing was taking place on the southwest shore near Hagushi, a feint was made by the 2nd Marine Division against the southeast of the island. By midday the Marines had taken the Kadena and Yontan airfields and by dusk around 60,000 troops had been landed. The majority of the Japanese garrison, waiting in the south of the island, remained hidden in the caves and dugouts of the Kakazu Ridge until the XXIV Corps turned in their direction on 4 April. After eight days of ferocious combat the Ridge and the Machinato Line were taken, but XXIV Corp's divisions could not press on immediately to attack the Shuri Line. On 4 May the Japanese commander, Lieutenant General Mitsuru Ushijima, launched a counterattack which failed to achieve its objectives at a cost of 5,000 casualties. In turn, Buckner now attacked the Shuri Line but progress was slow against a well planned defence in depth, and fighting was particularly intense on Sugar Loaf and Conical Hills. The critical moment of the battle arrived in the second half of May when the 96th Division took Conical Hill, forcing Ushijima to withdraw his troops to the Yaeju Dake Escarpment. By 14 June Buckner's divisions had begun to penetrate this position and within a week Japanese resistance had been reduced to a level appropriate to mopping-up operations. The cost of taking Okinawa had been high with 110,000 Japanese killed and 37,000 Americans wounded and 12,500 killed. At sea thirty-six American ships had been sunk and nearly 400 damaged. In the last American amphibious assault of the war the Allies had gained a close base for the invasion of the home islands. The Japanese, by their obstinate defence of that base had, unwittingly, provided a warrant for the use of the atomic bomb.

The strategic bombing of Japan before the spring of 1945 had achieved little significant result. As early as June 1944 the US 20th Bomber Command, based in India, was flying B-29 missions from advanced airbases in China against targets in both Japan and Manchuria. Their frequency was limited by the practicalities of resupply and their effectiveness by high altitude bomb runs, cloud obscured targets, and the fact that even at the limit of their range the B-29s could only strike the southernmost island of Japan, Kyushu. With the capture of the Marianas, Tokyo and Japan's industrial regions lay within range of the 21st Bomber Command, and from October 1944 attacks were concentrated on Japanese aircraft production. They were largely unsuccessful and a new tactic of comparatively low level incendiary raids was introduced in February 1945. As Japan's industrial zones and cities contained a high proportion of wooden buildings these attacks were more effective, and in a raid on Tokyo on 25 February B-29s dropped 450 tons of incendiary bombs which resulted in the destruction of an estimated 28,000 buildings. Even greater devastation was achieved during the night of 9–10 March when over 200 B-29s dropped nearly 1,700 tons of incendiaries on a heavily built-up section of Tokyo. The resulting fires destroyed approximately sixteen square miles of the city, killed over 80,000 people and burned out in excess of 250,000 buildings. Other major cities in Japan – Kobe, Nagoya, Osaka, and Yokohama – were subjected to the same tactics with varying, but at times almost equally horrific results. Japan's defences against such night raids were largely ineffective and less than 2 per cent of the bombers used in night missions were lost.

As a result of such raids Major General Curtis Le May, commanding 21st Bomber Command, believed that bombing alone could force the defeat of Japan and that an invasion would thus be unnecessary. Once the requirement for tactical bombing during the Okinawa Campaign was removed May was able to mount a sustained campaign against Japan from March to August 1945. Missions aimed at aircraft production and oil storage and

A Curtis dive bomber's view of the Japanese super battleship *Yamoto* trying to escape attacks by US Navy aircraft. The Yamoto with 18-inch guns, the largest battleship in the world, was finally sunk by a massive American air strike off Okinawa in April 1945.

A machine gun crew of the 6th Marine Division on Okinawa in June 1945 edges around a cliff to take aim at Japanese troops emerging from a cave opposite them.

refinement facilities achieved only limited success, but the incendiary raids on fifty-eight urban areas were frighteningly effective. Over two million buildings were destroyed, nearly 700,000 people were killed or injured and a further nine million made homeless. Although loyalty to the emperor remained strong, national morale was shaken by this very visible expression of American power and by the severe disruption to civilian life. Supplies of food and raw materials were also seriously affected by the naval blockade imposed around Japan. Sea communications with the southern area of the Greater East Asia Co-Prosperity Sphere had been severed early in 1945, but from April a close blockade of Japanese waters was mounted. In addition to the continuing operations by the Pacific Fleet's submarines, the 21st Bomber Command began long distance mine laying, and the Fast Carrier Force commenced raids against shipping in harbour and at sea off the home islands, while bombardment groups destroyed industrial installations with shell fire. From 17 July the British Pacific Fleet, now comprising three fleet carriers – *Formidable*, *Implacable*, and *Victorious* – the battleship *King George V*, and six cruisers, took part in operations against targets in Japan. With movement in the Inland Sea made hazardous by mines, with submarines operating at will in the Sea of Japan, and with the Yellow and East China Seas swept by air and surface forces, Japan was virtually isolated. The blockade meant that food for the Japanese population had to come from their own fields, and that supplies for Japanese industry had to come from whatever reserves were still held.

Although Japan's strategic war effort was finished, there were very real fears that her surviving armies, and indeed the Japanese people, would fight to the death if the Allies invaded the home islands. This collective, national suicide might, it was thought, cost upwards of one million Allied casualties. Planning for the invasion of Japan had begun in December 1944 and Operation OLYMPIC, the invasion of Kyushu, had been given a target date of 1 November 1945. This would be followed by CORONET, the assault on Honshu. With President Roosevelt's death on 12 April 1945, President Truman called for a reexamination of the invasion strategy and it was finally presented to the British and Russians at the Potsdam Conference in July 1945. The naval contribution to OLYMPIC would take the form of the US 3rd and 5th Fleets, with some British and Commonwealth support, while the landings would be carried out by the 500,000 officers and men of General Kreuger's 6th Army. The more important CORONET

This B-29B Superfortress was the aircraft flown by General Jamese Doolittle (of Dootlittle Raid fame) when he commanded the 8th Air Force in Okinawa. This version of the B-29 is the Challenger which was used in high altittude bombing missions over Japan. These bombers relied on speed and altitiude to evade enemy fighters.

landings, fifty miles to the east of Tokyo, were scheduled for 1 March 1946 with ground troops largely provided by the US 1st and 8th Armies. A Commonwealth corps of three divisions was earmarked for participation in CORONET invasion, while RAF bombers from Okinawa, and the British Pacific Fleet operated in support.

In the event, the invasion of Japan was not necessary. Faced with the massive slaughter of Allied troops and Japanese civilians that it was predicted an invasion would entail, President Truman and his advisers considered the possibility of dropping one or more atomic bombs on Japan. The Potsdam Declaration of 25 July 1945 had warned the Japanese Government that if they did not surrender, their country would face 'prompt and utter destruction'. In reply, the reputedly moderate Prime Minister, Admiral Suzuki, stated that Japan would ignore the declaration. This answer convinced Truman that whatever ethical and humanitarian problems surrounded the use of the atomic bomb, it would have to be employed in order to shock the Japanese Government into surrender. Shortly after 8.00 am on 6 August 1945, three B-29's from the 509th Composite Group appeared in the sky over Hiroshima, a Japanese city of 343,000 people. One B-29, *Enola Gay* piloted by Colonel Paul Tibbets, dropped an atomic bomb over the centre of the city. Within seconds an estimated 78,000 people were dead and a further 51,000 injured. The dropping of a second atomic bomb on Nagasaki on 9 August, as a result of which a further 66,000 people were killed or injured, served to underline the hopelessness of the Japanese position. As Prince Konoye had pointed out to the emperor in

The scene at Hiroshima after the explosion of the first atomic bomb on 6 August 1945.

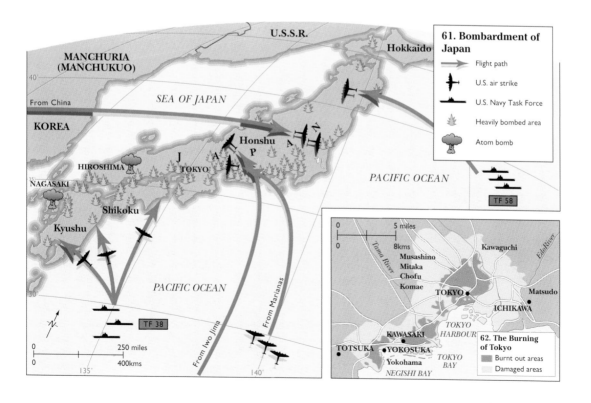

61. Bombardment of Japan

Flight path
U.S. air strike
U.S. Navy Task Force
Heavily bombed area
Atom bomb

62. The Burning of Tokyo

Burnt out areas
Damaged areas

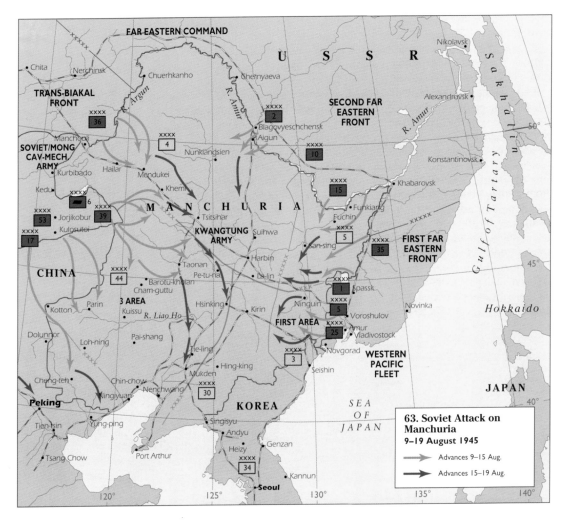

FAR EASTERN COMMAND

U S S R

Nikolavsk

Chita
Nerchinsk
Chuerhkanho
Chernyaeva

TRANS-BIAKAL
FRONT
xxxx
36

R. Argun

R. Amur

Blagovyeschensk

Aigun

xxxx
2

SECOND FAR
EASTERN
FRONT

Alexandrovsk

Sakhalin

SOVIET/MONG
CAV-MECH
ARMY
Kurbibado
Hailar
Mendukei

Manchooli

xxxx
4

Nunkiangsien

Khemi

xxxx
10

Konstantinovsk

Khabarovsk

R. Amur

Gulf of Tartary

Kedu
xxxx
6

xxxx
53
Jorjikobur
xxxx
39

xxxx
17
Kulosutoi

M A N C H U R I A

Tsitsihar

KWANGTUNG
ARMY
Suihwa

Harbin

Funkiang

Fuchin

xxxx
15

xxxx
5
San-sing

xxxxx

xxxx
35

FIRST FAR
EASTERN
FRONT

CHINA
xxxx
44
Barotu-kholan
Cham-guttu

Taonan
Pe-tu-na

La-lin

Ninguin

xxxx
1
Spassk

Novinka

Hokkaido

45°

Parin
Kuissu
3 AREA
R. Liao Ho

Hsinking

Kirin

FIRST AREA

xxxx
5
Voroshulov

Kotton

Dolunnor
Loh-ning
Pai-shang

xxxx
25
Amur
Vladivostock

WESTERN
PACIFIC
FLEET

Tie-ling

Hing-king

xxxx
3

Novgorod

Seishin

JAPAN

40°

Cheng-teh
Chin-chow
Nenchwang
Mukden

xxxx
30

KOREA

SEA
OF
JAPAN

Peking

Tien-tsin
Yung-ping
Singisyu

Andyu

Tsang Chow
Port Arthur

Heizy
Genzan

xxxx
34

Kannun

Seoul

63. Soviet Attack on
Manchuria
9–19 August 1945

→ Advances 9–15 Aug.

⟶ Advances 15–19 Aug.

120°   125°   130°   135°   140°

Soviet tanks, infantry, and
planes attack the rear of the
Japanese Kwantung Army in
the mountains in Central
Manchuria on 9 August 1945.

February 1945, Japan had to end hostilities. The willingness of President Truman to use the atomic bomb against Japanese cities, together with the Russian declaration of war, enabled the emperor to persuade the Supreme War Council that Japan should surrender. On 14 August 1945 Japan agreed to surrender unconditionally and, accordingly, hostilities came to an end on 15 August except in north China, Manchuria and the Kuriles where the Soviet Union was pursuing its own territorial objectives.

Although for the Allies Okinawa was the last significant land battle of World War II, the Soviet Union, with Germany now defeated, declared war against Japan on 9 August 1945. The Russians had signed a nonaggression treaty with Japan in April 1941, but they had confirmed at the Teheran Conference in November 1943 that they would prepare for hostilities in the Far East once fighting in Europe had ceased. The Japanese defence of Manchuria rested with the Kwantung Army which by August 1945 totalled some one million men deployed in twenty-four divisions and twelve brigades. Although a formidable force on paper the Kwantung Army had seen its fully operational divisions despatched to the Pacific and the bulk of its remaining forces were ill-equipped and inadequately trained. Its opponent, the Soviet Far East General Army Group, numbered approximately one and a half million men, many of whom had until recently been in combat in Europe. The Soviet force outnumbered the Japanese in tanks by five to one and in aircraft by over two to one.

The Russians attacked immediately after their declaration of war and exploited their armoured forces to the full. The 1st Far East Area Army located at Vladivostock advanced west to Harbin, and the Trans-Baikal Area Army moved east against Hsinking and Mukden. While these armies formed the Soviet striking force, the 2nd Far East Area Army moved south to eventually link up with the 1st Far East Area Army at Harbin. By 14 August the position of the Kwantung Army was desperate and it was only saved from catastrophe by the general ceasefire of 15 August. In a campaign lasting barely one week the Russians estimated that they had inflicted 80,000 casualties on the Japanese, while over 30,000 of their own troops were killed and wounded. Approximately 590,000 Japanese troops surrendered. At the same time as the advance into Manchuria, Soviet forces attacked Japanese 88th Division in southern Sakhalin by both land and amphibious assault, and fierce fighting occurred after Russian landings in northeast Korea. Hostilities continued until 22–23 August and in the Kurile Islands Russian amphibious forces continued operations until 31 August 1945.

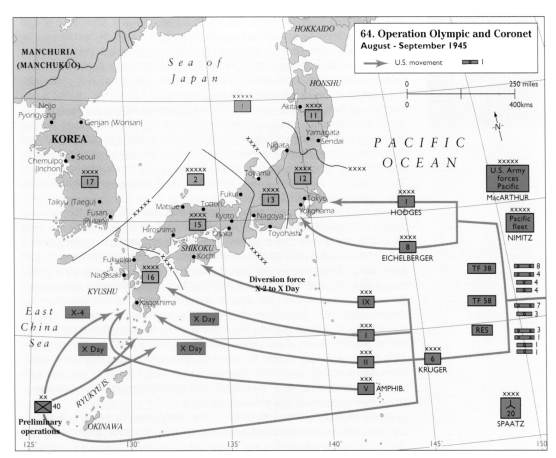

64. Operation Olympic and Coronet
August - September 1945

central Pacific showed.

Though the huge Japanese manpower losses were largely the result of this absolute willingness to die for country and emperor, Imperial General Headquarters and subordinate commands were excessively wasteful in their deployment of troops. Time and again Japanese units, both on land and at sea, were thrown into battle in inadequate numbers without any real hope of success. Even though US Marines had occupied strong positions on Guadalcanal, and were supported by air and naval units, the first Japanese attack designed to evict the marines from the Island was carried out by a single, lightly equipped infantry regiment. It failed by a substantial margin. Had attacks been delivered in strength and with coordination between the armed forces, Japanese manpower would have been conserved and an even heavier price exacted for the ground gained by the Allies. The Japanese logistical system was rudimentary in the extreme, particularly in the jungle, and it relied principally on what the individual soldier could carry. Once this supply was exhausted Japanese soldiers literally had to live on the country. With the enemy in close contact this was not always possible, and many Allied units found themselves engaging Japanese soldiers who were seriously weakened by exhaustion, malnutrition and disease. None of these conditions, by themselves, stopped the Japanese fighting, but the more sophisticated Allied medical and supply systems provided a significant advantage on the battlefield. In Burma, in particular, the work of the medical services was crucial. In the 14th Army during 1944, for example, there were 24,680 battle casualties, but 541,575 casualties from infection and disease.

A convicted Japanese war criminal is led to his execution at Changi Jail, Singapore.

The Allies enjoyed a marked technological superiority during the war in the Pacific, particularly in the latter stages. American and British technology when deployed on the battlefield or at sea tended to perform as expected; Japanese technology often did not. Nor did the Japanese keep pace with developments in the enemy camp. Japan's war economy, already stretched to breaking point by its attempt to compete with the industrial capacity of the United States, had perforce to concentrate upon quantity rather than quality. Although they began the war with a superior fighter in the Zero and a more effective torpedo, the Japanese were unable to maintain such qualitative supremacy as the United States switched to a national war footing. In fields such as radio and radar the Japanese fell far short of the quantity, reliability, and sophistication of the equipment issued to their forces by the Allies. Japanese ocean going submarines, for example, lacked radar and were equipped with only rudimentary sonars. By 1945 the Americans could call upon helicopters for pilot rescue, could use penicillin in the treatment of infection, and could apply nuclear fission to warfare.

The United States developed two fundamentally important strategic weapons during the war in the Pacific: the carrier task force and the fleet train. By removing the US battlefleet from the war for some months in December 1941, the Japanese also removed the possibility of battleship tactics continuing to dominate American thinking at the aircraft carrier's expense. Henceforth there was no alternative to basing naval tactics on the carrier task force. Thereafter not only did the United States carriers defeat the Japanese Combined Fleet, they also provided the platform from which amphibious assaults upon enemy held shores could be mounted. The only way that surface fleets could remain within range of land based aircraft during such assaults was by having a stronger air umbrella, either carrier or land based, themselves. Thus Task Force 58 (Fast Carrier Force) and Task Group 52.1 (Support Carrier Group) were able to operate off Okinawa for over two months, without losing a single ship, only because they could sustain their own air defence. With the Kamikaze the Japanese made a last ditch attempt to counter the advantages the carrier task force gave the Allies. They failed but they were able to inflict substantial havoc before the war ended. For example, Task Forces 58 and 57 (British Pacific Fleet) between them had twelve carriers, four battleships, and a number of lesser warships damaged during the Okinawa operations. The destructiveness of the Kamikaze was blunted by effective air defence, and by the use of radar picket destroyers to provide warning of approaching attacks.

It has been claimed with some justice that the bulldozer was one of the decisive factors of the war in the Pacific. Certainly this versatile item of equipment, when placed in the hands of the 'Seabees' of the US Navy construction battalions, contributed an immense amount to the building of airfields and bases. A bulldozer could conjure an airstrip from the unpromising terrain of the islands and archipelagos of the Pacific in a matter of hours, thereby enabling air support to be brought into the front line. If carrier task forces were diverted to other duties this provision might mean the difference between success or failure in an amphibious operation. Similarly, the momentum of the advance across the Pacific would have been severely compromised without the support provided by the At-Sea-Logistics Service Group. Such a group consisted of oil tankers, tugs, and supply and repair ships which could maintain both themselves and a combat fleet at sea for many weeks. As a result, the United States could sustain the maximum naval power at the crucial point of a campaign, and could also extend their

An Allied prisoner of war in a physical condition typical of most prisoners held by the Japanese.

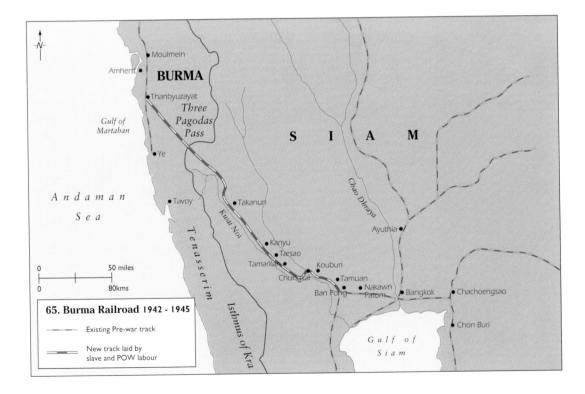

65. Burma Railroad 1942 - 1945

——— Existing Pre-war track

═══ New track laid by slave and POW labour

operations into areas beyond the range of land based support.

The United States was able to use its submarine force to strangle Japan's seaborne communications and to destroy a large proportion of the shipping which provided a vital supply link between the territories of the empire. The Japanese, who were wedded to the concept of using submarines almost exclusively in support of the Combined Fleet, were ill-prepared in training and doctrine for the prosecution of an anti-shipping war. Whereas American submarines operated in the western Pacific throughout the war, Japanese boats withdrew from the eastern Pacific at an early point in hostilities. Despite a disappointing start during 1942, and the inadequate performance of the Mark XIV torpedo and the Mark VI magnetic exploder, American submarines sank in excess of 1,300 Japanese vessels totalling 5.3 million tons. These losses meant that Japanese garrisons became increasingly isolated, that the power of the Combined Fleet was constantly declining, and that the industrial capacity of the home islands was progressively starved of imports.

The corollary of the Japanese abhorrence of being captured was their

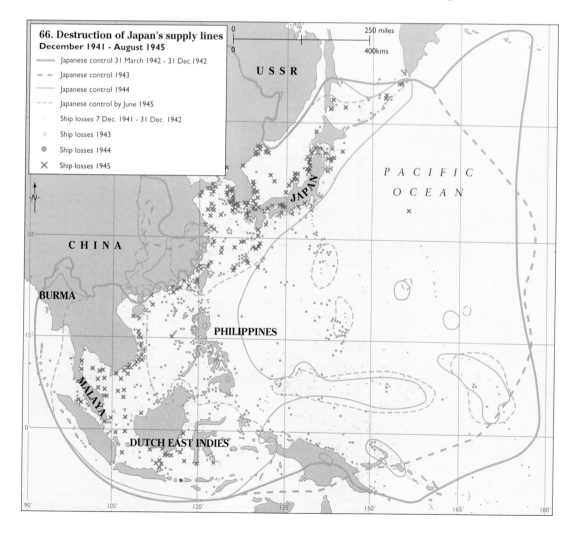

66. Destruction of Japan's supply lines
December 1941 - August 1945

— Japanese control 31 March 1942 - 31 Dec. 1942

- - Japanese control 1943

—— Japanese control 1944

- - - Japanese control by June 1945

· Ship losses 7 Dec. 1941 - 31 Dec. 1942

◦ Ship losses 1943

● Ship losses 1944

✕ Ship losses 1945

deep revulsion for anyone who had allowed himself to become a prisoner of war. This revulsion was worked out, against both military and civilian prisoners, through physical punishment which embraced many states from beatings to torture and execution. The Japanese were the guardians of nearly 200,000 Allied prisoners of war. The majority were men and women who had been captured in the first six months of hostilities, as the Japanese swept through Hong Kong, Malaya, the Philippines, Sumatra and Java. Many did not survive to be liberated in 1945. Of 20,000 members of the United States forces captured in the Philippines in 1942 nearly half died in Japanese camps. Of the 60,000 Commonwealth prisoners of war who struggled to build the Burma-Siam Railway, over 12,000 died before its construction was completed. Of the 2,500 Commonwealth prisoners held in 1943 at Sandakan Ranau in North Borneo, only six survived. A proportion of prisoner deaths were caused by the fact that the Japanese used their labour to support the empire's war economy. Many fatalities, however, were due to deliberate neglect, to the inability to provide an adequate diet and medical supplies, and to calculated and deadly brutality. At the end of the war, in trials in Yokohama, Singapore, Manila and other centres, the British and Americans tried 2,329 people as war criminals and convicted 2,040. Of these 428 received the death penalty.

General Homma of Bataan Road fame in Yokohama Prison awaiting trial in November 1945.

A US Navy submarine "somewhere in the Pacific" in 1945. American submarines were not one of the casualties of Pearl Harbor. They quickly gained ascendancy in the Pacific and were able to attack Japanese shipping more or less at will.

The signing of the formal surrender of Japan aboard the battleship USS *Missouri* in Tokyo Bay on 2 September 1945.

Bibliography

The following works have been particularly helpful in the preparation of this book:

Allen, L. *Burma. The Longest War 1941–45*. London, 1984

Cutler, T J. *The Battle of Leyte Gulf 23–26 October 1944*. New York, 1994

Evans, D C, ed. *The Japanese Navy in World War II*. Annapolis, 1969

Firkins, Peter. *The Australians in Nine Wars. Waikato to Long Tan*. Sydney 1982

Foster, S. *Okinawa 1945. Final Assault on the Empire*. London, 1994

Fraser, David. *And We Shall Shock Them. The British Army in the Second World War*. London, 1983

Fuchida, M and Okumiya, M. *Midway. The Battle that Doomed Japan, the Japanese Navy's Story*. Maryland, 1955

Hagen, Kenneth. *This People's Navy. The Making of American Sea Power*. New York, 1991

Kirby, S W *et al*. *History of the Second World War. The War Against Japan*. Vols 1–5. London, 1957–1969

Garand, George and Strobridge, Truman. *Western Pacific Operations. History of U.S. Marine Corps Operations in World War II*. Vol 4. Washington, 1971

Long, Gavin. *Australia in the War of 1939–1945. Series One. Army. Volume VII. The Final Campaigns*. Canberra, 1963

Love, Robert. *History of the U.S. Navy 1942–1991*. Harrisburg, 1992

Millett, A R and Maslowski, P. *For the Common Defense. A Military History of the United States of America*. New York, 1984

Morton, Louis. *United States Army in World War II. The War in the Pacific. Strategy and Command: The First Two Years*. Washington, 1962

Prange, G W. *At Dawn We Slept. The Untold Story of Pearl Harbor*. New York, 1991

Shaw, Henry *et al*. *Central Pacific Drive. History of U.S. Marine Corps Operations in World War II*. Vol 3. Washington, 1966

Slim, Field Marshal the Viscount. *Defeat into Victory*. London, 1956

Smurthwaite, David ed. *The Forgotten War. The British Army in the Far East 1941–1945*. London, 1992

Spector, Ronald. *The American War with Japan. Eagle Against the Sun*. New York, 1985

Index